HELEN RICE
The Great Lady of Chamber Music

by Rustin McIntosh

Printed in the United States of America

By the George Little Press, Inc., Burlington, Vermont

Binding by New Hampshire Bindery, Concord, New Hampshire

Library of Congress Catalog Card Number: 83-72885

———————————————

FOREWORD

In his Foreword to Edwin T. Rice's MUSICAL REMINIS-CENCES (1943), Walter Price spoke of the outstanding *individuality* of Helen Rice's father: "What he thought, he said; what he said, he lived. His opinions might be at variance with those held by others, but always with gentleness and becoming grace he gave the evidence of his own opinions, relying upon his knowledge, his experience, and his conviction....... He long ago discovered that the finest of the fine arts is the art of living. In it he saw contentment and understanding, and the joy of appreciation in art.''

Helen's mother was a beautiful and gracious hostess to New York's musical leaders, making the Rices' home a warm and stimulating gathering place for those who shaped New York's musical life.

Helen Rice added to these qualities of distinction, inherited from her parents, a cosmopolitan outlook and a deep sense of caring for individuals. Where her father's music journals list chamber music participants by a few dozen, Helen's music diaries record over a thousand. A gracious hostess like her mother, she preferred informal entertaining, thus freeing herself to focus on the basic interests of her life: people and music.

The following pages are testimony to her gift of friendship and kindness, and to her unique contribution to the world of chamber music.

Ruth McGregor

ACKNOWLEDGMENTS

Many people participated in this tribute to Helen Rice. In addition to those friends who wrote letters and sent pictures, the following individuals made a special contribution of time and effort:

Jacques Barzun with his kind suggestions of possible publishers; Louise Behrend who coined the phrase used in our title; Mildred Hagler who deciphered many difficult handwritings for the letter section; Samuel Hayes for support in financial and practical matters; Susan Lloyd for her keen editorial eye and good judgment; Rumsey McGregor for typing lists and making uncounted trips to the Xerox center; Ruth McGregor for compiling the results from Helen's music diaries; Millicent McIntosh, Helen's lifelong friend, for her sound advice and wisdom; Rustin McIntosh who sacrificed hours and days from his beloved garden to catch the essence of Helen's life on paper; Edwin T. Rice II, Helen's cousin, for furnishing family pictures and records and for photographing the two William Rice portraits that formerly hung in Helen's New York apartment; and Donald Spuehler, Chairman of the Amateur Chamber Music Players, whose legal advice and interest encouraged this labor of love.

The Editors

Cover Design

The cover design was drawn by Richard B. Snow from a music cabinet in Helen Rice's studio. Helen had commissioned Robert Lloyd to design and build the cabinet, using motifs reminiscent of a favorite of hers in the Metropolitan Museum.

CONTENTS

Helen's maternal grandfather,
Ogden N. Rood

Helen's paternal grandfather,
Edwin T. Rice, Sr.

Helen's grandparents, the Ogden N. Roods and Edwin T. Rices

BIOGRAPHY OF HELEN RICE
by Rustin McIntosh

Helen Rice was born on October 16, 1901 at 71 Central Park West in New York City. When she was a year old her parents moved to a newly built apartment house at 15 West 67th Street, which was her residence for the rest of her life. She died there on April 22nd, 1980, at the age of 78. New York City was thus the chief geographical focus of her life — this and Stockbridge, Massachusetts, where her maternal grandparents had built a house in 1874 and where Helen spent most of her summers.

Portrait of Helen Rice as a child by William Rice
Kindness of Edwin T. Rice II

1

There were notable lovers of the arts in Helen's ancestry. Her paternal grandfather was a member of Dartmouth College's Handel Society in the 1840s and became its organist in his Senior year. At a later time he and six other members of his family sang in the New York Oratorio Society. Her father, Edwin T. Rice, was an enthusiastic amateur cellist who over the years invited scores of musicians to his home to take part in sessions of chamber music.

Portrait of Helen's mother, Margaret Rood Rice, by William Rice
Kindness of Edwin T. Rice II

Helen's father, Edwin T. Rice   Helen Rice age 3

He not only had a wide acquaintance among professional musicians of his time, but as a practising lawyer had as clients the Flonzaley Quartet and the Kneisel Quartet. He served on the board of directors of the Symphony Society of New York, later of the New York Philharmonic Symphony Society, as well as that of the Institute of Musical Art, later the Juilliard School of Music. He was also the recipient in 1936 of the Elizabeth Sprague Coolidge Medal for eminent services to chamber music. An uncle, William M. J. Rice, was a portrait artist of some distinction.

On her mother's side, her grandfather, Ogden Nicholas Rood, professor and head of the department of physics at Columbia University, was the author of a textbook* on color and color perception which is said to have had considerable influence on painters of the time. An uncle, Roland Rood, an older brother of Helen's mother, was also a practising artist and the author of a book.

For Helen's father, chamber music was a vital element of life, a virtually essential ingredient. The apartment to which he moved his family in the autumn of 1902 had a large living room two stories high, ideal for recitals and small concerts. There he adopted

---

*Modern Chromatics: Students' Text-Book of Color with Applications to Art and Industry, Ogden N. Rood (1831–1902), including facsimile of the first American edition of 1874. Preface, introduction and commentary notes by Faber Birren, New York, Van Nostrand Reinhold Company. Copyright 1973 by Litton Education Publishing Inc.

3

the custom of inviting musical friends once a week or even oftener, their talents so distributed that with him as cellist they constituted a string quartet or perhaps quintet. Professional musicians and amateurs were included. In his own hand Mr. Rice kept a log recording not only the names of the players at each session but also the compositions played. Their programs ranged widely, almost each session including some new work. He had a standing order with some of the music publishers in Europe to send him new compositions that showed promise. It is quite probable that a number of works were given their first performance in the western hemisphere at these informal meetings; this is almost certainly true of Schöenberg's Verklärte Nacht, Florent Schmitt's piano quintet, Chausson's concerto for piano, violin and string quartet, and for the Enesco octet.

Helen began taking violin lessons at an early age, and soon, under the tutelage of so experienced a teacher as Edouard Dethier, had made enough progress to justify her being included as a participant in one of her father's musical evenings at home at the age of fourteen, when her name first appears in his records. For her, however, this somewhat forced introduction to ensemble playing was a not unmixed blessing, for it made her uncomfortably aware of her technical immaturity. Long afterward, in retrospect, she confessed that the anxiety and lack of assurance that accompanied these early efforts made her far more unhappy than her father was aware of. It was only in later years that her love of chamber music blossomed.

In early life Helen had a German governess, so that it is likely that she spoke German before she did English. She retained a comfortable competence in spoken German throughout her life. Thanks to French classes at the Chapin School, through visits to Europe, and especially to the French-speaking part of Switzerland, and after Bryn Mawr by means of graduate study in Columbia University, she became proficient in spoken French.

Her attendance at the Chapin School in Manhattan began at age 6 in 1907. Her athletic ability soon came to the fore, as did her developing personality, and by the time she reached her Senior year, in 1919, she was elected "Head of School."

Her four years at Bryn Mawr College, class of 1923, brought her again into prominence as an athlete; in field hockey she was on her class team all four years, on the varsity team in her Senior year; captain of her class water polo team in her Freshman and Junior years, and on the varsity team in both her Junior and Senior years; on the swimming team all four years; on her class basketball team for the last three of her college years; captain of her class tennis team in her Freshman year, a member of that team and also of the varsity team all four years, and college champion in both Freshman and Senior years. In her final year she was President of the Athletic Association.

In those days music at Bryn Mawr was at a remarkably low level, and Helen's skills along those lines were not mentioned in her class yearbook. She received her A.B. in June of 1923 with the rest of her class. President M. Carey Thomas is reported to have said that Bryn Mawr had no chapter of Phi Beta Kappa for the good reason that a bachelor's degree from Bryn Mawr was the equivalent of Phi Beta Kappa in any other college.

After college, what? Helen felt no call to enter graduate school. Her later participation in courses in Columbia's French Department was brief and limited to her desire to sustain her competence in that language. Her father was strongly opposed to her finding a job; in the eyes of most men of his generation "work" was unladylike. For a long time she was content to travel, to visit with friends, practice the violin, play some tennis, enjoy a well-earned rest.

5

In Paris 1925

In June of 1924 she sailed to Europe, reaching Paris on the 20th. After a two weeks' visit to Belgium, a tour of that country supervised by her friend Avis Dethier, she returned to Paris, bought a bicycle, and undertook a tour of Brittany very much on her own. By the end of July she had gone to Switzerland, meeting with old friends, the Rothen family and Mlle. Favre. In August she joined her parents in Zurich and took part in a tennis tournament. Seeing new places, meeting up with friends and relatives, she roamed through Austria, Bavaria, Brittany, the Loire valley, the south of France, Italy, and back to Switzerland for Christmas; then to Paris again for some courses at the Sorbonne, a tour of cathedral towns, music lessons with Nadia Boulanger; again to Switzerland, meeting her mother in Zurich, eventually sailing on the Leviathan, arriving in New York in early September of 1925, having been abroad for well over a year. In the autumn of 1925 she resumed field hockey, playing on the New York team in a variety of intercity matches. But this, plus French and violin lessons, concerts, theater, and visits with friends, was not enough to satisfy a social conscience.

After a "heated discussion" with her father in the spring of 1926 on the subject of jobs, Helen undertook some part-time volunteer work at the Henry Street Settlement and Trade Union League. Reading between the lines of her rather sparse diary, one gets a sense of her dissatisfaction with a life of almost totally hedonistic pursuits. She spent some time in Blue Hill, Maine, taking violin lessons, practising, playing in quartets, picnicking.

In January 1927 President Marion Park of Bryn Mawr invited her to serve as Warden of Radnor Hall for three months, April through June, to fill the position of someone who was to go on leave. With Helen's strong loyalty to her alma mater, the offer was not one to be easily refused, and she thoroughly enjoyed this short renewal of college life, with its opportunity to take part in sports, to come to know a new set of young friends, even to encourage the instrumentalists among them to join in sessions of chamber music. It was the sort of work that carried with it the dignity of a job, yet met her father's objection that by accepting it she would be displacing some potential breadwinner who needed the position more.

In January of 1935 she joined the Cosmopolitan Club in New York, a means of meeting with old friends and making new ones, a congenial organization in whose activities she shared throughout the rest of her life. Over the years she made a notable contribution to its activities by organizing from time to time groups of volunteers to offer informal chamber music concerts — "members' concerts" — in the library or the ballroom.

Georgette Baer and Helen at Delphi

7

In the course of additional trips to Europe she invariably homed in on the Rothen family in Switzerland, renewing her strong friendship with Mme. Rothen of the older generation and with her coevals, Georgette and Alexandre. Georgette became perhaps her closest friend outside of the United States; she played at the wedding when Georgette married Dr. Baer, a distinguished biologist at the University of Neuchâtel. Later Helen was godmother to the Baers' daughter Anne-Tillie, sent the latter many gifts, and attended the wedding when Anne-Tillie married M. Jean Sahli. Both Georgette Baer and the Sahlis have visited Helen in New York and Stockbridge. Alexandre Rothen, who qualified in medicine and spent several years in research at the Rockefeller Institute, sought a tennis game with Helen whenever it could be arranged; they were very closely matched.

In 1938 Helen was again invited by President Park to be a warden, this time of Rhoads Hall, and she again accepted. In contrast to her earlier, short-time stint, she now put considerably more effort into arranging programs of informal music, an activity to which the college had meanwhile become notably more hospitable. With the approval of the Music Department she was given an official title, Leader of Chamber Music. She held these positions for four years, through the academic year 1941–42 when she resigned. It was during these years at Bryn Mawr that she played quartets quite frequently with a particular group of amateurs — Catherine Drinker Bowen, the author, and the brothers Alwin and John Pappenheimer, scientists then working at the medical school of the University of Pennsylvania; all three were to become lifelong fast friends.

The death of Helen's father, in February 1940, brought her closer to her mother, but at the same time increased her freedom to organize musical evenings among her own friends.

The Rice family were staunch supporters of the New York Symphony from its founding until 1927, and later of the New York Philharmonic Orchestra. Helen continued her father's subscription to parterre seats after his death, right up to the time of her own death. She also subscribed to and attended the New York concerts of the Philadelphia Orchestra in the 1960s and '70s with her friends Ruth and Rumsey McGregor. Her knowledge of symphonic literature was therefore extensive and her taste catholic. She was indifferent to the symphonies of Bruckner and Mahler, and she never became an opera fan.

In the summer of 1940 Helen joined the faculty of the Greenwood Music Camp, which had just moved to new quarters in Cummington, Massachusetts. This is a summer school for children roughly between the ages of 11 and 18 who have a special interest in chamber music. Helen taught violin and played first violin in the faculty quartet (with Bunny Little, second violin, Margaret Clark, viola, and Ruth McGregor, cello). This group rehearsed every afternoon and played once a week for the children. In addition Helen coached chamber music groups among the campers, coached tennis, and managed in her spare time to construct pine tables and benches for use on the dining porch. Even after she resigned her faculty position in 1946, she continued to visit Greenwood and to play for many years; she also served two five-year terms on the camp's Board of Trustees.

At Greenwood 1946   *At Miss Backus's farm*

A major interest of Helen's was gardening, both flower and vegetable, but especially the latter. The land around the Rices' house in Stockbridge was too shaded to support much besides lilies-of-the-valley and periwinkle, which it did in profusion; but there was invariably some friendly neighbor whose property included more garden space than the owner alone could manage, and Helen was always welcome to take over a plot. If woodchucks, rabbits or raccoons threatened, she rigged her own electric fencing. She planted a wide variety of items, just about everything that was known to thrive at the latitude of Stockbridge — everything, that is, except potatoes; she somehow shared the all too current belief among women that the potato is in general to be avoided. Helen liberally passed along samples of her produce to her host and to friends near and far, besides of course keeping her own kitchen well supplied. She did especially well with raspberries and grapes, cultivating varieties of each, so that she was able to provide fresh fruit for a long season.

Beginning in 1942, when the nation was on a war footing and when meat and gasoline were rationed, and everyone's efforts were directed so far as possible into useful channels, Helen spent more time in Stockbridge and more energy in raising fruits and vegetables. She enlarged her garden and periodically took a generous load of produce to the Greenwood camp. It was in those years too, when farm labor was particularly scarce, that she undertook to help a neighboring dairy farmer by sharing in the twice-a-day milking routine, for which of course she accepted no pay.

Helen was an early and enthusiastic member of the Berkshire Garden Center, located at the intersection of Routes 102 and 183, about a mile distant from her home. At their annual money-raising harvest festival, usually held in October, she was well known for always providing pounds and pounds of home-made fudge, which was invariably sold out to the last cube. It would be interesting if one could calculate the total value of her gift to the Garden Center over the years, for she continued her fudge ritual even in the last year of her life before her final illness had produced its first symptom.

Another dominant interest of Helen's, as has already been made clear, was tennis. From an early age she was coached by her mother on the courts of Stockbridge's old Casino, now defunct. The game took with her, and she soon showed innate talent. At the age of 11 she and her mother won the ladies' doubles at the Greenock Country Club in Lee, Mass. At 14 she won the ladies' singles championship in the Stockbridge Country Club adult tournament. At the age of 17, while still at the Chapin School in New York, she competed in the first annual girls' junior (i.e., under 19) Metropolitan lawn tennis championship tournament held on the courts of the West Side Tennis Club at Forest Hills on Long Island, winning the singles title and, teamed with Miss Winifred Aydelotte of California, also the doubles title. The next year she successfully defended her singles title and, again with Miss Aydelotte, the doubles.

Her tennis career at Bryn Mawr has already been described. After college, tennis became her chief sport; she and her mother repeatedly won the ladies' doubles event in the annual Berkshire Hills tournament. At one time or another she had played against well-known opponents, for example, Albert Spalding and Pablo Casals. Men who considered themselves pretty good tennis players were apt to find her a really tough match, with an uncanny ability to keep the ball in play. She played a not particularly aggressive game, but had the knack of keeping going until her opponent made an error; and she was always keen for the game. Slowed down in the 1950s when a benign tumor in one calf required operative removal, she finally gave up tennis in the 1960s when degenerative changes in a hip joint began to produce symptoms.

Another avocation was cabinetmaking. At some time in the 1930s, apparently from a desire to pursue a constructive occupation, Helen took lessons in carpentry and began making pieces of furniture. Through her wide acquaintance with workmen of various trades in Stockbridge she succeeded in locating a number of chestnut boards, taken from big trees that had succumbed to the chestnut blight which struck throughout the United States in the first decade of the century — some of the boards a bit worm-eaten, to be sure, but still prime material for the construction of sturdy articles of furniture. A special product of her craftsmanship was fireplace benches, one of which she gave to the present author and his wife in celebration of our purchase and recondi-

Helen at age 17, winner of girls' junior Metropolitan lawn tennis championship tournament at Forest Hills
Credit N.Y. Tribune

11

tioning of an old farmhouse in Tyringham, a few miles from Stockbridge. It is 35 inches long, 12 inches wide, and stands 13½ inches high, its two posts ornamented by scrollwork of Helen's design. It is one of our most highly prized possessions, has weathered beautifully the passage of nearly half a century, and has withstood the onslaught of ten grandchildren, each of whom considers it his or her special seat. It is but one of several which Helen is known to have built. Some of this cabinetwork was done in her bedroom in New York, most of it in her parents' house in Stockbridge, and all without benefit of power tools. In a small ledger kept in her desk are listed 69 separate items, including bench, book case, book ends, book stand, cabinet, candlesticks, footstool, hearth brushes, lamp table, magazine stand, music stand, piano bench, suitcase stand, tea table, and tool rack. At least the initials of the person to whom she gave each item are listed, but no dates. It is doubtful that she found time for this sort of work after 1947 when she undertook to be secretary of the Amateur Chamber Music Players.

In the use of tools Helen took after her mother, who was first rate at minor household repairs. Her father, on the other hand, was far from handy with a screwdriver.

In 1945 Helen was invited to be head of the Music Department of the Brearley School, an independent school for some 500 girls from kindergarten to college entrance, located not far from Helen's own school, the Chapin. This was a challenging opportunity, like nothing she had been asked to do previously; and to make it even more stark, she was to succeed a much older woman, Berta Elsmith, of impressive talents, whose specialty was choral singing and "putting on" operas. Overcoming her misgivings, Helen accepted the position, trusting to her firm background in musicianship and realizing that she could grow with the job, as indeed proved to be the case.

At the start there was only one string player in the entire student body. Being an ardent chamber music player herself, Helen at once introduced a string program into Class V, where every girl was given a six-week introductory class in either violin or cello, in groups of four. She asked her old friend and Greenwood Camp associate, Ruth McGregor, a cellist of broad experience, to teach this course with her on a part-time basis. In time, fostered by Helen's enthusiasm, the course encouraged some of the girls to study the instruments in private lessons, and soon there came into being a Brearley Ensemble with students and faculty participating. Indeed, the course became a model which other independent schools followed. Helen invited outside players to play chamber music for and with the students, both in classroom and at assemblies. Ever since then the Brearley has had a fine instrumental program.

In addition to conducting large choral groups, Helen taught the college entrance level course in history and appreciation of music, for which her qualifications were beyond question. Her best students, with whom she established lasting friendships, were usually given Advanced Placement credit in their applications for admission to college. At last Helen had found a job which was truly productive and which involved her lifelong interest.

Carleen Hutchins with Helen

It was during this activity at the Brearley that she became a close friend of Carleen Hutchins, at that time science teacher in the Lower School. A budding and enthusiastic violist, Carleen declared at one point that she thought she would like to make a viola. This so astonished Helen that she blurted out "If you manage to turn out a playable viola, I'll eat my hat." With this challenge Carleen went to work and with determined persistence over the course of many months and the expenditure of acres of sandpaper, did indeed produce an instrument which proved to be not only playable but a thing of beauty in itself. True to her word, Helen baked and decorated a cake in the form of a small straw hat, and invited Carleen and a couple of dozen friends, including of course the Brearley's music staff, to an evening party by way of celebration. The viola was played in demonstration by Louise Rood, a distinguished member of Smith College's music staff. Carleen, who no longer teaches at the Brearley, went on

13

to make not only more and even better violas but the whole family of viols, all eight of them from treble violin to contrabass, and to devote her career largely to scientific investigation of the resonance of stringed instruments. Helen retired from her position at the Brearley in 1950, having in the meanwhile found herself challenged to take up another career which proved even more to her liking.

Helen wearing the hat made of cake

Helen eating her hat, with Ruth McGregor and Louise Rood

14

The ideal job for Helen, as things turned out, proved to be the secretaryship of the Amateur Chamber Music Players, which gave rein to her love of music, especially of chamber music, her boundless capacity for friendship, and her profound desire to be of service in a good cause. Briefly told, the origin of the ACMP was as follows: A business executive of Indianapolis, Leonard A. Strauss, an enthusiastic violinist, whose work involved a good deal of traveling, saw how welcome it would be if there were some way of finding in a strange city fellow musicians who would enjoy playing string quartets even with a complete stranger, provided he shared their enthusiasm and could hold up his part. Consulting by letter with a few musical friends around 1946, he found them encouragingly responsive. He even wrote in this vein to Catherine Drinker Bowen, the writer, whom he had never met but whose book "Friends and Fiddlers" indicated that she might well be of like mind — as indeed she was, replying promptly with the confession that she had always wished there was some national directory by means of which she too could find amateur musicians with similar leanings. It was she who suggested that he write to Helen Rice. In March 1947, an informal organizational meeting was held in the Rices' apartment in Manhattan, attended by Helen, her mother, Leonard Strauss, Catherine Drinker Bowen, Robert Haven Schauffler, another writer, Maulsby Kimball of Buffalo, Ruth McGregor of New York, and a few others. Helen volunteered to be secretary. From that point a list of amateur chamber music players, or putative members of an association, was in the making. It was agreed that anyone who wanted could join; there were to be no dues, but contributions were encouraged. The list would grow by members' letting their like-minded friends know of the organization's existence.

It was soon agreed that members would set their own evaluation of technical competence, grading themselves either A (excellent), B (good), C (fair), or D (etc.); and since a number of professional musicians wished also to join, a fifth category, Pro, was added. The first directory, published in 1949 by the National Association of Amateur Chamber Music Players, as the organization first called itself, contained 1,200 names, confined to residents of the United States and Canada. Since then, the group has shortened its name to Amateur Chamber Music Players, or ACMP, Inc., and is authorized to receive tax-deductible contributions. Growth has been rapid; the second directory contained a few hundred more names and included residents of Mexico as well as of the United States and Canada. Currently, the North and Central American Directory containing a few thousand names of instrumentalists and singers is published every two years, alternating with the Over-Seas Directory, also issued every two years.

ACMP's first overseas member, Dr. Carlos Vollenweider of Argentina, with the then treasurer and secretary

The first Over-Seas Directory, containing the names of members in South America, Europe, Africa, Asia, Australia and New Zealand, appeared in 1968; a recent sequel contains about 750 names and includes 48 countries. Each member of ACMP receives a copy of the directory in which his or her name appears and may request the other current directory. The association also distributes an annual newsletter with a financial report, rough estimates of growth in membership and geographical extension, and selected accounts of members' experiences in satisfying their musical longings through use of the directory.

During the first several years of ACMP's existence the secretarial burden borne by Helen Rice was indeed formidable. She personally answered all inquiries, usually writing letters in her own hand, since she was not a trained typist, and treating each new member as a personal friend. An inquiry by telephone often led to her inviting a complete stranger to join in a session of chamber music at her apartment in New York or at her home in Stockbridge. Such invitations were extended especially freely after her mother's death in 1960 when Helen became mistress of both establishments. The pleasure she derived from participation in chamber music and from these secretarial activities designed to promote participation on the part of others afforded some compensation for her having to give up tennis and to cut down on the amount of time and physical energy she could by that time devote to gardening. Cabinetmaking had long since been crowded out.

Over the years, the number of people who have joined with Helen in playing chamber music can be tallied not merely by dozens but by hundreds. For each such fortunate individual her eminence as a leader in the field stands out bright and clear. She had the technical skill to cope with any violin part, and the sensitivity and musicianship to exploit its potential. Her knowledge of the literature of chamber music was comprehensive and, in respect to string quartets and quintets in particular, detailed and accurate. As first fiddle she was an effective leader, but she gladly played second violin if someone else preferred to take the lead; and she could also take a viola part whenever called upon. It gave her particular pleasure to introduce young musicians to the charms of ensemble playing, and she had a notable gift for inducing bashful or self-conscious young musicians to join in group play, often with the result that a new and unanticipated enthusiasm was kindled.

By 1965 the appreciation for what Helen Rice had been doing for chamber music, and for the members of ACMP in particular, had become so vocal that a movement sprang into being to celebrate her by giving her a surprise dinner party — if the secret could be held. In the spring of 1965 potential participants were sounded out, and the ballroom of the Cosmopolitan Club reserved for a particular evening in October; but the response was so massive that within a short time far more acceptances had been received than those facilities could accommodate. The reservation was consequently canceled and arrangements made to hold the dinner in a more spacious facility. All members of ACMP were invited, by letter or telephone, and always with the urgent appeal to keep the matter a secret. The flood of acceptances presented problems.

Helen was told only that she must reserve the evening of October 29th for a dinner with friends "at the club." The author had the pleasure of escorting her from her apartment; and before the taxi had gone far she protested "But this isn't the way to the Cos Club." When we arrived at the Esso Building on West 51st Street, she was immediately surrounded by a group of her intimate friends, one of whom draped around her neck a lei of white carnations which had been flown from Hawaii especially for the occasion. The secret was out by then, but the size of the gathering continued to amaze Helen as she entered the reception hall. Some three hundred musicians did attend the dinner, several from foreign countries (Israel, Portugal, Venezuela), some meeting Helen for the first time though known to her by correspondence. The en-

Guest of honor at the 1965 ACMP dinner

tire ACMP had been urged, whether they could come or not, to write a message expressing their appreciation of Helen's service as secretary of the organization. These tributes — letters, telegrams, prose and verse — were placed in a specially made leather portfolio which was presented to her as part of the dinner ceremony.

Samuel P. Hayes, then chairman of the Board of Directors of ACMP, served as master of ceremonies and invited the participants to take their places in the dining room. At the head table with Helen and Mr. Hayes were the speakers — Catherine Drinker Bowen, Dr. Virginia Apgar, Jay Rosenfeld, music critic of the *Berkshire Eagle,* and Dr. Rustin McIntosh. Congratulatory telegrams from Justice Abe Fortas and Mr. Henry Simon, publisher, were read. After affectionate and touching tributes to Helen on

Rustin McIntosh, Samuel Hayes and Helen with Catherine Drinker Bowen on the dais

18

the part of the speakers it was a severe challenge to her to be invited to respond. Of course she met it with courage, grace and tact, expressing her thanks to the Dinner Committee and to the entire membership of the ACMP as well as to the actual participants.

Following the surprise dinner party, musical activity at 15 West 67th Street increased if anything. There were apt to be quartets or quintets two or three times a week, the variety of players, if not also their number, increasing. As her father had done before, Helen kept a record of all the chamber music activities that took place in her home, including the names of the participants and the compositions played. These ledgers, one for each year from 1930 to 1980, were carefully preserved.

A device of special usefulness in enabling Helen to bring together large numbers of musicians of varying (and sometimes unknown) technical competence is what came to be called a "Brandenburg evening," or simply a Brandenburg. It began with her inviting some twenty or so friends to join in the ample music room of her New York apartment to play a few compositions for small orchestra — for example, Bach's Third Brandenburg concerto, or his concerto in D-minor for two violins and orchestra, or perhaps some of Handel's concerti grossi. The first trial was a resounding success. Skilled players enjoyed the larger numbers and the wider range of dynamics, as well as the charm of the compositions themselves. Less experienced players were thrilled to participate, to be dragged along by their musical betters and made to play better than they knew. Before long the device was repeated, the range of compositions extended, new instruments added such as winds and horn, permitting the program to include such items as the Bach suites and the 4th and 5th Brandenburg concerti. The 6th Brandenburg concerto also became a great favorite. Some quite distinguished musicians often took part, sometimes conducting, at other times playing the solo parts or simply joining in with the rest. With Helen's extraordinary library there was no dearth of compositions from which to choose an evening's program. By tradition each session began with J. S. Bach's Brandenburg concerto no. 3 for a warm-up, whatever was to follow. Helen invariably offered refreshments after these musical barbecues: ginger ale (her favorite drink), beer, cookies, and delicate sandwiches which she had prepared earlier in the day. No participant would be likely ever to forget her sandwiches.

In her zeal to encourage chamber music Helen would often arrange special sessions involving beginners, sometimes quite young children who had only recently taken up a stringed instrument and who might never have played with a group. With the help of a few tolerant grown-ups, sometimes parents, sometimes friends with an equal fondness for children, she would start a timid group on an easy movement of a Haydn quartet, perhaps, or an early Mozart. With her engaging enthusiasm, and mustering huge tolerance for mistakes, she would launch a group on what was to them a quite novel experience, opening ears and eyes to the joy of participation. For ever so many, such an introduction under Helen's guidance opened the path to a lifetime of enjoyment. A friend who had helped out in a number of these sessions for fledgling musicians estimated that quite possibly Helen had played Eine kleine Nachtmusik as many as a thousand times.

David McGregor (left), 10, holds music sheet as group, calling themselves the "Christmas Bell Ringers" rings out a song in front of the Morningside Drive residence of President-elect Dwight D. Eisenhower in New York City Dec. 25, '52. While their bells rang out Christmas tunes the Eisenhowers were inside entertaining guests. Anna Strauss, second left, with Helen and assorted Paynes and McGregors.
Credit Wide World Photos

Another gambit she often employed for involving numbers of people was bell-ringing. The Chapin School had a set of English hand bells with a range of about an octave and a half, accurately tuned and of beautiful tone quality, which could be used by a group of eight or more persons to play hymns, chorales, Christmas

20

songs and other short pieces. With music written in large characters on a big sheet of cardboard placed on a music stand or perhaps held by a non-player, the group would form a semi-circle, each person holding one or two bells and so placed as to have a clear view of the score. Even a child who had never been taught to play an instrument could quickly recognize "his" note or notes, corresponding to the bell or bells he held, and could see where to come in. Initial performances were, of course, always rather rough, but with repetition the playing became smoother and the sound more pleasing. Some of the bell-ringing sessions were held in Helen's music room, either in New York or in Stock-bridge; others took place al fresco, especially in the Rockefeller Center area during Christmas week. Crowds would quickly gather; presently a police officer might turn up with a tolerantly amused expression, or perhaps he might feign alarm at the size of the crowd and ask the group to move to a different location. Clearly the music added to the Christmas spirit and was welcomed by passers-by. These outdoor sessions were traditionally topped off with hot chocolate at Schrafft's. Early in the bell-ringing game Helen borrowed the Chapin set; later she teamed with her friend Anna Lord Strauss to buy a second set,* of which Helen acted as custodian.

For most of her life Helen was fortunate in enjoying excellent health. At some time in the 1950s she began to experience pain in her right hip which led to consultation with orthopedists and the identification of degenerative arthritis, with the prospect of increasing pain and disability. Medication was only partly helpful. In time there was some shortening and she walked with an increasing limp despite constant use of a cane. Just at this time the operation for replacement of the hip joint came on the horizon and Helen gave due consideration to the possibility of having to resort to it; but the advice of one of her doctors — "postpone it as long as you possibly can" — appealed to her and she elected to do without. To her surprise and that of most of her advisors the pain came under ready control, shortening ceased, and though she continued to walk with a decided limp she could get along almost as fast as ever. The possibility of operation was dismissed forever.

---

*Anna, before her death, left her share of the bells to Helen, who deeded them to Anna's niece, Janet Knauth.

However, something more formidable was in store. Beginning a short time before Christmas 1979 she was troubled with an unproductive cough and loss of appetite. Early in 1980 x-ray studies showed a lesion in one lung which on surgical exploration proved to be a malignant tumor, its primary site not identifiable. Further surgery and radiotherapy in these circumstances were out of the question. She was offered chemotherapy, with the possibility of prolongation of life but at the price of almost certain severe distress; she wisely refused. Fortunately she continued to be free from pain, but the illness took its irrevocable course, with complete absence of appetite and progressive weakness. Her friend Ruth McGregor stayed with her to the end. She died slowly, quietly, peacefully.

Helen was not religious in a conventional sense. Although she often played in various churches when requested to do so for the benefit of some evening program, she was not an active church member. While she did not believe in "the resurrection of the body and the life everlasting" and other parts of the Apostles' Creed, her life and work were dominated by the Golden Rule. She was generous to all, and to her friends invariably ascribed generosity in both motive and deed.

Virginia Apgar with Helen

Helen playing trios with Ruth McGregor and Mariana Barzun

It remains to mention a few of her particularly close friends who died earlier and whose friendship was important in her life: Dr. Virginia Apgar, anesthesiologist and student of the respiratory problems of newborn infants, in the last years of her life Medical Director of the March of Dimes, a violist whose boundless enthusiasm bridged whatever gap might lie in her technical competence; whenever she visited, her help in the kitchen lightened the load and always left more time for music. Catherine Drinker Bowen, historian, author of several remarkable books, an eager chamber music player, always ready to join whenever a quartet could be brought together, but who invariably insisted on playing second violin. Warfield and Janet Longcope, who moved to Lee when Dr. Longcope retired as Professor of Medicine at Johns Hopkins, on whose superb tennis court Helen played countless games. Katharine Strauss Mali, Bryn Mawr classmate and lifelong friend, and her sister Anna Lord Strauss, poetry critic, editor, and past president of the League of Women Voters, at whose home Helen had Thanksgiving dinner year after year. Jay and Beth Rosenfeld, whose home in Pittsfield harbored chamber music throughout the year. Joseph Stein, of Belmont, Massachusetts, perennial host to musicians and supporter of all chamber music ventures. Mariana Lowell Barzun, top flight violinist with whom Helen particularly enjoyed playing. Eunice Wheeler, of Worcester, able violist with whom Helen played as often as possible and who deeded her Gasparo da Salo instrument to the Performing Arts School of her home city.

An innate gift for friendship like Helen's is all too rare, especially when it is unprejudiced, unselective. She had close friends from all walks of life and in various parts of the world. She met new acquaintances with open and engaging warmth. Not that she failed to recognize cant when she met it. There were times when she suffered fools because failure to do so would have caused hurt feelings; but a fool once identified was not given a second chance. She could be severe when she detected selfishness, and thoughtlessness also got black marks. For her friends, whom she held to be the salt of the earth, she could not do enough.

Rustin McIntosh

LETTERS AND TRIBUTES

The Board members of the Amateur Chamber Music Players decided to publish a biography of Helen Rice after a Questionnaire circulated among its members indicated their enthusiastic approval. In a subsequent Newsletter members were invited to write letters for inclusion in the following section. With the help of Helen's address books, friends outside of the ACMP were invited to send their reminiscences also. It was understood that the letters would be edited and excerpts used. In a very few cases, clearly indicated, letters written *to* Helen before her death are included and dated.

Molly Rockwell and Helen at the Corner House in Stockbridge 1976

My first memory goes back very far, but it has imprinted itself on my mind. It was an incident that startled me into thinking I was in fairyland. Suddenly I looked at a familiar tennis court, and there was a little, light-footed and gay curly-haired girl, playing against a tall and obviously skilled lady, flying over the court and holding her own. I was entranced, and stopped for some time watching them.

It was some time later that I found out it was Helen Rice and her mother, neither of whom I had seen before.

Several years later, I watched Helen playing against a young man. That was a very serious match, and I saw the particular expression with which I became familiar when she was corralling all her strength and skill.

Honors came to her in tennis. Once she was sent as a junior representative of some organization. I asked her if she would make tennis her major interest, but she said: No, she had sometimes thought so but, one day when she was playing in Europe, in a pause in the game she heard her challenger whistling one of the later Bach concertos. She decided on the spot that not tennis, but music, must have first place. She never changed that decision.

Because I am very ignorant in music, particular memories are less sharp in that field, and all come together in much gratitude for her kindness in giving me opportunities to hear music of many kinds, and patience with my ignorance.

There are many clear pictures and I have chosen only a few:

Helen, in a rare winter trip to Stockbridge, reveled in the snow. We took a snowshoe walk on Yale Hill where she gloried in the view of the mountains, and did not know that she herself was a fine picture of appreciation.

We both had a taste for berries. I see us walking down the rows of unbelievably big raspberry bushes in Helen's beloved garden; or on a mountain top, crouched among the blueberry bushes, rejoicing in the sun and the berries we ate as we picked.

When I asked to borrow her station wagon to transport some old-fashioned hair mattresses to a place in Bridgeport, which remade them, she bethought herself of her own throughout the house. I can still see the station wagon, loaded with mattresses from floor to ceiling, and to savor the good talk we had.

One August evening she shared with me a special sight that she had found, looking for fireflies, which she loved. She took me to a meadow glittering with numberless flying sparklets. Suddenly my mind's eye saw again the little fairy girl dancing on the tennis court, and I marveled that a seeming fairy had become a most wonderful friend.

Molly Rockwell
Stockbridge, Massachusetts

To write about Helen is to write about a friendship (lasting over 60 years) which began in September, 1914, when I arrived as a "new girl" at Chapin, and Helen took me under her wing. She had arrived two years earlier when her parents heard of the Saturday Playground Program and, therefore, opted for Chapin rather than the Brearley they had been considering. Preliminaries were simple in those days, and Helen reported waiting in the hall with her father the day school opened. It was athletics then that brought her to Chapin, and coming in as an athlete she became and remained our leading one throughout her school career. At the same time she participated in a wide range of other school activities, leading to her election as Head of the School in our 12th class (senior) year 1918-19.

Looking back at school years, they seem almost idyllic . . . small classes, usually interesting, related wherever possible to current events (for example, in March 1917, when news of the Russian Revolution reached us, we discussed with Miss Chapin whether it could avoid the pitfalls of the French Revolution), pleasant relationships between the teacher and the taught, minimal tensions and plenty of "extracurricular activities."

These were war years, and Eastern seaboard sympathy was markedly pro-Ally, yet friendships were hardly disturbed by this. Nor did the war encourage any anti-German hysteria. The Fräuleins remained with us, and German classes continued. In November 1918 the fire alarm at one o'clock, as we were about to go home, brought emotional relief with the news of the false armistice preceding the real one some ten days later. Graduating in 1919, with a solid education, considerable idealism, and the war behind us, we moved on from school to college to meet new challenges, "fortiter et recte." In the fall, Helen and I went down to Bryn Mawr escorted by my father. At Bryn Mawr, Helen was drawn rapidly into athletics and undergraduate affairs. She was one of four temporary presidents for the entering freshmen and President of the class the following year.

Helen, who had majored in languages, spent the year '24-'25 in Paris where I joined her in 1925. She was living chez Mlle. Guillemin on the rue Delambre and, as her hostess was away, she was doing the marketing and cooking. I dined with her the night I arrived, after which she put me back on the metro and told me where to get off, urging me to learn public transportation and not be just a tourist. To this day I remain quite at home on the metro!

Blissfully unaware that we belonged to a "lost generation" and equally unaware of any Great Gatsby syndrome, we explored the city and its environs, revelling in the beauty we saw. Helen led me blindfolded ("Shut your eyes, Fran, shut your eyes,") up from the dark ground floor of the Ste. Chapelle so I would appreciate the full glory of what was above. That summer, our friendship with the head of the French Department at school, Mlle. Favre, who once referred to Helen as her "grammaire vivante" and to me as her "traductrice en chef," led to our meeting Mlle. Favre's family in Geneva, and Helen's long and affectionate association with her niece, Georgette Baer, who lived many years in the lovely country above the Lake of Geneva, in which Helen delighted.

Our fiftieth Chapin reunion Helen insisted should take place at her apartment, as she was the only person living where she did when she was in school. For some, this was reminiscent of the Rices' gemütlich household — Mrs. Rice's numerous cats, and her sunny window of plants which Mr. Rice called her "bugonias." Helen was Helenchen and called her father Neddie. Years later, unencumbered by cats, Helen regularly took her plants from New York to Stockbridge and back again.

There were later memories, too, of the Amateur Chamber Music evenings and, for me, an initiation into bellringing one Christmas afternoon, when everybody counted aloud and shouted, "Fran," when I was to ring my bell. At the reunion, Helen added a personal note, telling us that some 37 countries had been represented at gatherings in her New York apartment, where music transcended all language barriers.

When asked to speak on a French theme at one of the Cosmopolitan Club Members Luncheons in 1977 (still a bicentennial year), I asked Helen to introduce me. This apparently delighted her. In the process of working it out together, friends for over 60 years ourselves and knowing our parents had been friends as long, Helen discovered our grandparents had also been friends. Her grandfather, Ogden N. Rood, Professor of Physics at Columbia, known for measuring the spectrum had, Helen noted, "written a textbook on color with the artist much in mind." Presumably this brought him into contact with the Impressionists of the day and with my grandfather, the painter John LaFarge, a sensitive colorist, working also in stained glass. Hence, at the memorial for Professor Rood at the Century Association, shortly after his death in 1903, LaFarge spoke appreciatively of him. "Honored to say something in praise of a man whom I admired and for whom I had much personal liking," and stressing the importance of science to the artist. To this Helen added,

"Doubtless it was this mutual interest that brought these two gentlemen together."

Looking back over our years of friendship when our paths converged or diverged and reconverged according to our interests and activities, it was always fun for us to be together.

Frances Childs
New York City

Her family and mine had been friends through three generations. I still remember never-resolved arguments between our mothers: mine marvelling at Mrs. Rice's ability to raise an only child successfully; hers impressed with mine for having coped with six.

I played a certain amount of tennis with Pudd'n, [Helen's college nickname], from 1920 on, never as a winner unless on her side of the net — but what happy recollections of a teammate whose most virulent expletive, at her occasional bad shots, was "Oh, sugar!"

We were both Freshmen representatives in the Bryn Mawr delegation to Silver Bay in 1920. This included a fair share of athletic competition — swimming and tennis — which must have tried the generally prevailing Christian spirit to the utmost. Because not surprisingly Pudd'n won everything.

Ruth McAneny Loud
New York City

Letter written to Helen October 8th, 1965

Dear Helen,

"So many memories come up: the great high studio-living room with all those paintings on the walls; quartet-players seated under the lamp, your father faithfully among them at his cello, your lovely mother whose good looks and kind ways played their part in the ensemble of the surrounding atmosphere; and later, the Brandenburg evenings with such an array of stands and lights and players; and later still, the get-togethers for the KdF*. I see you always against this background, and when I think of what you have stood for in your own personal sphere and what you have accomplished in spreading the general feel of it all in the ACMP, I marvel at you and am aware of how content your father would be to know how you have carried on the tradition, what you have done, what you have brought about."

Polly Crena de Iongh

1980

Helen cast a great light on the music world and it shines not only on the Amateur but also on the Professional world. It is a light that will never be extinguished.

Polly Crena de Iongh
New York City

*Kunst der Fuge, edited by Polly (Herter Norton) and Roy Harris for string quartet.

I think I first got to know Helen in the early 1930s. I played quartets with her often until I moved to Armonk in 1936. What a joy those quartet sessions were.

Later, she included me in many of her Brandenburg evenings. Her hospitality is famous. What a good time she gave everybody!

The members' concerts at the Cosmopolitan Club were organized by her. They, too, are highlights in my musical life and association with Helen. She enjoyed people, and was very good at getting together people that would enjoy each other. All who knew her are indebted to her for many delightful times.

These last few years, I always looked forward to at least one lunch with Helen at the Members' Luncheons at the Cos Club. She didn't make our last date in March of 1980. She wrote me a touching "farewell" letter, reviewing our friendship and making no reference to her terminal illness. What a lady!

Emily Hadley
Armonk, New York

In Switzerland Noël 1966

We met in 1922 in Geneva (Switzerland) where she had come to visit a dear retired French teacher who had taught her at Miss Chapin's school.

She had golden curly hair, a melodious voice, an air of distinction and a charming smile.

We soon became friends. It was a happy time — bicycling, mountain excursions, music (Nardini concerto!). Everyone she was introduced to loved her. She adapted easily to our simple way of life, happy to leave the grand hotel at which she had been staying.

She was strong physically as well as morally, played tennis, won a tournament with a kilo of chocolate as a prize (quickly disappearing she said). Quite independently, she went to Greece, to Italy. On summer holidays, seven of us young ones went on the Alps. We slept in a primitive chalet; mattresses were made of big bags filled with dry leaves and . . . fleas. How we envied Helen wearing pyjamas (quite unusual for Swiss girls at that time); she quietly tied her trousers around her legs, her sleeves around her wrists and went asleep. As she had taken her violin with her, rainy days were the source of recitals (romantic music which made us nearly cry with emotion!).

In 1928, despite her suffering from seasickness, she came back and played on my wedding day in the chapel of the cathedral.

Then we met again in Paris where she took violin lessons. Many reminiscences come back, too many to speak of. I just want to quote this one: As we were in a bus at a stop, passengers began to laugh. When Helen discovered the cause of this hilarity (a drunken man discoursing in the street), she said loudly, "Je ne trouve pas ça drôle." Immediately the laughing ceased.

She returned to New York, her father having written and said that he disapproved of Americans living abroad and avoiding their responsibilities towards their country.

Later, when airplanes had taken place of boats, she came back to Europe; to Switzerland (Saint-Blaise, Corseaux, Zurich), to France (Juan-les-Pins), to England and Greece again.

Her enthusiasm for chamber music was contagious, she transmitted the virus to the young generation.

It is impossible to say all that Helen did in Stockbridge and elsewhere (gardening, cow milking, etc.). She never got up after 8 o'clock, no matter how late chamber music had gone on the day before. It is impossible to say either what she was, the elevation of her mind, her kindness, her comprehension of others. She was a lady, she was a friend.

Georgette Baer
Corseaux, Switzerland

———————

In 1938 while attending the second Berkshire Festival at Tanglewood, I ran into an acquaintance from my home town, Worcester, who was in Stockbridge for a tennis tournament. On asking her who her next rival was to be, she answered "someone by the name of Helen Rice." Having met Helen briefly in New York ten years before when she and I, along with Bunny Fay Little (later of Cummington's Camp Greenwood fame), were all students of Edouard Dethier, I sent through this friend my greetings to Helen. That same day came a message to the hotel inviting me and whoever was with me to come to a quartet session that evening at her house. Thus burgeoned a 42-year friendship which changed my life completely — as the lives of untold thousands have been changed through Helen's 33 years as dedicated (voluntary) Secretary of the Amateur Chamber Music Players.

In New York and in Stockbridge her unique brand of hospitality was open to friends and strangers alike — from quartet weekends of convivial friends to launching young talents before a carefully selected audience of experts. She initiated the joys of chamber music at her alma mater, Bryn Mawr; hostessed annual "Brandenburg" evenings, as well as "Greenwood" reunions. She pushed a new group activity by investing in a set of English hand bells, and at Christmastime ringing in the holiday spirit in hospitals and even on a busy street corner one year until a traffic jam broke it up! She made frequent trips to Europe to promote memberships in the ACMP. This organization was officially recognized as beneficial to international relations, even occasionally leading to international marriages! She was not only an energetic traveller for the ACMP, but made out of her vast correspondence a very personal relationship which was chiefly responsible for the organization's fantastic growth all over the world.

Nor was her deep involvement in music to the exclusion of other interests. Perhaps her second "love" was her garden in Stockbridge from which she produced all kinds of vegetables and flowers which she shared with her many friends. She was a worker and great supporter of the Berkshire Garden Center there. As one of her contributions during World War II she took on full care of a cow — I think her name was "Ricie"? — housed at Stockbridge "Town Farm," milking her twice daily. She loved animals!

Helen with "Ricie" at Miss Backus's farm

Whether on formal or informal occasions, her conversation was always interesting and informative and her diction impeccable. In 1965 a big surprise party in her honor was given by the ACMP and her extemporaneous response was beautifully given.

One cannot enumerate all these varied interests of Helen's without mention of her devoted friend and quartet partner, Ruth McGregor, who both encouraged and shared so many of Helen's activities right up to the end of her life.

Eunice Wheeler (dec.)

re-printed from The Catgut
Acoustical Society Newsletter of 1980

There are so many happy memories of Helen that it is hard to sort them out. Of course music stands out first and foremost. The evenings in the high studio at 15 West 67 Street — looking down from the balcony at the musicians below or being one of them. Listening, enjoying, participating in every moment. Later in the evening, delicious food appeared miraculously — and good talk always.

Then there are the memories of Stockbridge and Tyringham, Helen teaching Tonio Palmer, the McIntoshes and other small fry tennis. Helen always gay and competent and immensely generous. Generous with her music, her time, her tennis and her delicious vegetables. Helen in her Stockbridge kingdom where good music, good food, good company and the glorious view combined to create a unique atmosphere — and to leave delightful memories.

It is good to know that her friends are carrying on the fine work of the Amateur Chamber Music Players launched by Helen. This is a true and living tribute to her generous "life and works."

She was by her mere presence a redeeming element of the human race — a joy to be with — truly a breath of fresh air.

Francesca Gilder Palmer
Rosamond Gilder
New York City

On the Palmers' court in Tyringham

My earliest memories of Helen are her many visits to our tennis court in Tyringham, to help me and my siblings learn to play the game. She was so patient, kind, and encouraging as we struggled to return the balls. These same qualities were also evident in her quartet playing with beginners. I also remember her excitement when she first took up the viola.

One amusing little story comes to mind when we brought Bernard Robinson, the British physicist and violist, from Boston to Stockbridge. He had come over mainly to see Helen the Fall before she died. At the dinner table he brought out a small present for her. None of us could make out what it was. He had to explain that it was a very special and extremely accurate metronome he had *made* for her! She turned to him with a twinkle in her eye and said; "Bernard, are you suggesting that I *need* to use one?"

Hylie Pappenheimer
Cambridge, Massachusetts

In Stockbridge, especially in the middle years of her life, Helen played a unique role in the life of my aunt, Grace Nettleton. When Helen started to spend more and more of her time in Stockbridge she began, in a small way, what proved a most absorbing and rewarding activity — the raising, harvesting and distributing of her own homegrown vegetables. Her own home on a hillside above the village offered no garden space, but my aunt, a friend of Helen's mother since their girlhood days in Strockbridge, was delighted to give Helen free rein in the Nettleton garden. The garden, well developed on extremely fertile soil, constantly enriched over a period of many years, was under the care of one Marshall Wright, a New England "Old Timer," originally employed by my grandfather Nettleton and well ensconced in his proprietary position, knowing what should or should not be done, and *stubborn,* but limited in his labors by the infirmities of advancing years. Helen, with great tact and understanding, became after a long trial period accepted by Marshall and did more and more in the garden, eventually taking over when Marshall was no longer able to work. She made a beautiful picture as she worked, dressed in the appropriate garb of a laborer, bending over with grace and ease to hoe and weed, against a background of rolling hills and brilliant blue sky.

Not only supplying the Nettleton home, Helen shared the produce generously with a large group of friends. I so well remember seeing her drive off in a large station wagon loaded down with vegetables for delivery and marvel at how much she accomplished in a few hours' work without apparent fatigue or loss of enthusiasm.

The garden brought Helen to the Nettleton home almost daily, often more than once a day. She always had time for a visit with my aunt, always a ready listener to family and other news, of practical assistance in meeting large and small problems, and taking on errands, the delivery of messages and anything else a close family member would undertake. Helen too brought her own news and shared many things of interest with "Gracie," as she came affectionately to address my aunt. Helen had the freedom of the Nettleton home and served as a co-hostess for many visiting friends, making it possible for them to see the beauties of the area and to share in the many artistic offerings, including with special delight the musical evenings in her own home.

Helen became a friend to Miss Backus, a long-term neighbor of the Nettletons, who was struggling alone, with very inadequate hired help, to maintain a small dairy farm. Helen, as part of her volunteer war effort, undertook the twice-daily milking task, and incidentally helped Miss Backus in other ways.

It is as a most thoughtful and attentive friend to my aunt that I feel especially indebted to Helen, but I also owe her much for the enrichment of my own life which came through her sharing with me the beauties of the Berkshire countryside, the warm, friendly gatherings in her own home, the delights of walks through the Nettleton woods, the climbs up Monument Mountain and the many occasions when we discussed light and serious subjects, while enjoying the joys of the outdoors or the comfort inside our homes. I shall always remember with gratitude the warmth of her friendship — a truly "giving" person.

Grace Bourne (dec.)

Milking at Miss Backus's farm, 1943

I cannot really remember the first time that the Knauth family rang the bells with Helen (we called her Pudd'n Rice, following the style of my mother-in-law, Marjorie Knauth, and her sisters, Anna Lord Strauss and Katharine Strauss Mali). The bells were always part of Thanksgiving celebrations at the Hattertown farm home of Anna Lord Strauss. They would come in with Helen in the two white suitcases which even then looked as if their days were numbered. We would feast at the long tables set up to run from the dining room well into the living room, would have a flurry of clearing and cleaning while some of the diners would stroll down Castlemeadow Road to the lake in the distant view. Then all would assemble in the living room to play and to listen. From the time they were able to hold a bell safely, Alison, Jennifer and Marianna and their cousins on the Mali side, as well as John's sister, Mary Knauth Field's three boys, Christopher, William and Gregory, were encouraged to ring along with the adults. It was among their earliest musical experiences and became very special to all of them. First there would be the practice changes, with Helen pointing to individual notes for the many who could not read, then "We Gather Together," and last a preview of Christmas with some early carols.

Truly, the combination of clear bell music in the late afternoon with the intent young faces and the equally intent faces of those who had rung for years, is a special memory which evokes Helen for me. Her gentle firmness and evident love for the music we were mutually creating was a gift to us all.

Suffice it to say the Thanksgiving tradition continues and we rejoice.

Janet Knauth
Rowayton, Connecticut

My childhood memories of Helen are tinged with awe, and with a certain ruefulness: sometimes I wondered if I could ever measure up to the standards she set for herself and others, and thus I felt, at times, too self-conscious in her presence to be my own best self (whatever that might have been). That she was so obviously my parents' friend and peer strengthened her character as judge. However, none of this prevented my responding gratefully

40

to her warmth and her hospitality, or to the wonderful simplicity of her respect for me as a person, a respect I saw her granting impartially to other friends of all ages. Nor did this background awe eliminate youthful audaciousness. The earliest example of such that I can remember occurred at the Friday afternoon chamber sessions over which she presided at the Brearley School for several years. I guess I was between eight and ten; my playing was pretty feeble, and I was participating as much because I ought to as because I wanted to. I was in rebellion against the key of B flat major, and I tuned down my E string a handy half-tone. This worked marvelously for almost fifteen minutes: others struggled with their fourth fingers while I blandly played open strings. Then we were asked to pause and retune. I snuck E flat back to E natural, then back again to E flat. Unfortunately, Helen noticed the second motion. Though her criticism was matter-of-fact and reasonable, I took it as an archetypical warning against childish shenanigans, and never really felt comfortable with her in earnest rehearsal until I was in my thirties. This discomfort didn't matter much for practical purposes, because we seriously rehearsed together on only a few occasions, the most notable be-

Sue McIntosh Lloyd and brothers Carey, Ken, Dick, and Jim

ing the summer I was sixteen or seventeen, when Helen took Carey, Jim and me in hand and introduced us to late Beethoven — Opus 135, I think — in a series of "coached" sessions at Tyringham. Those were exciting, stretching occasions. During an early rehearsal, I remember her saying that she could forgive herself (and, by implication, us as well) one mistake, but not the same mistake made twice over. "You can apologize once," she said.

Most of our playing together was for fun: with Helen arriving at Tyringham after afternoon milking during war years, in her eternal wooden station wagon, then later in her blue metal station wagon. She was never too busy to take a walk with Dad around the vegetable garden; supper was even more civilized than usual with all of us on our best behavior. There was music, ginger ale (I liked her smiling aversion to alcohol), and for me, sometimes, the hostly privilege of helping walk her out to her car in the dark.

I recall Helen resplendent in crimson velvet or other 1920's gown, welcoming us to a children's chamber orchestra party at her New York apartment. She must have played the first fiddle part for the *Eine kleine Nachtmusik* (and I the second) a hundred times. I feared but also enjoyed the obligatory greeting to her mother, who, from her height, was always polite. I remember being moved by Helen's warm, real gratitude for a small plant I had brought to her mother when Mrs. Rice was in her last illness; somehow Helen's response — a passing on of her mother's gratitude — gave meaning to all those formal transactions that had passed, inadequately, for conversation between me and Mrs. Rice all those years. I believe Jim had a genuine friendship with her. However, Helen's response to my gift brought to life my own relationship with Mrs. Rice, and impressed me with the uses of good manners.

By her own modesty, Helen dispelled all my barbarous envy of those who played better than I. Sometimes she played second violin; always others played the solos in these kid-sessions. Listening to other players, respecting their interpretations, appreciating effort even when results were dim: all these elements of chamber music manners I gradually absorbed and made my own — with no showing-off of my progress, because show was, of all things, to be deplored. Everything in Helen's dress, manner, and surroundings made this point, almost as though she was trying consciously to make it, as part of the education of "the young," as she called us. Her lovely old furniture, darkening yearly behind New York's unwashed windows, the very reeds in the vase the same, I believe, from one year to the next, her outmoded clothes, which I loved for their outmodedness — everything about and around her said that people and music mattered more than anything. Of course my family's values had well prepared me to appreciate this. Yet my friendship with and admiration of Helen made me proud to defend her refusal of fashion even to my mother, who appreciated its meaning at least as much as I did, but knew it colored some colleagues' perceptions of Helen.

Accomplishment mattered too. Helen's skill on the tennis court made her an exemplar as well as a legend in my family, though I was still more impressed with her skill at milking cows. I never once wondered why she didn't marry; I just assumed that no one had been good enough for her. And nature mattered. Since I carried to a passion her enjoyment of blueberrying and walking expeditions, I recall much undemanding happiness in the expeditions she arranged, or shared with us. I think she took us on our first family cherry-picking trip.

As I grew more adult, Helen shared with me many unvarnished opinions (usually of other people, but always in service of ends other than gossip). It took a lot to provoke her, but once provoked, she was not forgiving. We never talked of intimate concerns or personal problems — hers or mine; however, I feel certain she would have wanted and tried to help if I had ever needed her in this way. I don't ever recall laughing uncontrollably in her presence — or doing anything uncontrollably in her presence — but I remember with particular pleasure her delight at my (or our) accounts of the youthful excesses — musical and other — of the first Naushon house party in December, 1952. She and I carried on a steady correspondence, writing at least three or four times each year until her last. Some of this was by way of her communicating her appreciation — and that of ACMP members — of my Newsletter drawings (Helen was both polite and practical), but her letters were much longer and richer than politeness alone might suggest.

I was always touched by the way she cheered my family-of-marriage along. She gave us $200 as a wedding present to be spent on music (and we used every penny). Much more important, she took quickly to Bob, in spite of his originality and his un-McIntosh-like traits, appreciating that I appreciated these qualities (among others more conventional), and really admiring his designer-carpenter's eye and hand. One of the pieces he made for her was her stereo cabinet. She carefully showed him what she had in mind, producing photos of a carved choir screen (we think that is what it was) to show how she wanted the gleaming, modern speaker units contained. He gave her an estimate of $180 for cost of labor plus materials, fearing it was too low, but feeling he should not charge more for a stereo cabinet. Sure enough, he spent more than twice the time he'd optimistically projected, some of it learning to carve leaves and whorls. She wrote him that she was stunned by the results and enclosed a check for $300, explaining that she felt she should *pay* for the results, and knowing from her own woodworking experience what it had meant to turn out those cabinet doors.

Helen also took a warm interest in our sons as they arrived and grew. She came over to Tyringham especially to visit me and Ben a week after he was born. She enjoyed and encouraged their progress in music. They, like their mother, found reservoirs of politeness in themselves that they had never suspected when we visited her to ring bells or to play together. Her image is strong in their imaginations.

My last chance to play with Helen came in the summer of 1979 when, with Hylie and John Pappenheimer, she and I worked together to prepare Haydn's Opus 20, #4 for a benefit concert for the Tyringham church. She said this would be her last public performance; I don't know whether it was or not, but she spent some time chiding herself, and deplored her loss of fine left hand and bow control. She practiced very hard to make up for it. For that reason, it may have been a mercy that she died so soon afterwards.

Sue Lloyd
Andover, Massachusetts

I met Helen for the first time in 1923, I believe, in Geneva. It was her first trip abroad and she was traveling with a friend of hers. Helen had come to Geneva to see my aunt, Miss Daisy Favre who had taught her French at Miss Chapin's School. I must say that I was very much impressed with this young American girl who spoke a pretty good French whereas at that time my English was miserable. We went sightseeing in the old part of the city, even climbing the numerous steps leading to the top of the cathedral of the city of Calvin. On our way back to our apartment on the Quai des Eaux Vives with a most magnificent view

Alex Rothen with Helen

on the lake, I bought some pastries for tea, unfortunately in the wrong shop. The cakes were awful but Helen in her kindness thought they were marvellous.

A few years later, Helen was again in Geneva, in December that time. Now on the 11th of December the people of Geneva commemorate what has been called "l'Escalade", that is, their victory in 1602 over the Duke of Savoy, Charles Emmanuel, who in a treacherous attack had unsuccessfully attempted to take Geneva, at night, by surprise. For two days the inhabitants of Geneva are allowed to walk the streets "disguised," carnival fashion and they go visiting their friends. Helen was very much interested in taking part in the festivities, and I lent her some Swiss military trousers to contribute to her costume. She was simply delighted and the evening was quite successful. Fifty years later both of us remembered vividly this celebration of the "Escalade" of 1602.

Helen was interested in so many things besides chamber music. She was kind enough to enquire about the progress of my scientific endeavors and was truly interested in my results. She probably had inherited some "scientific" genes from her grandfather, a physics professor at Columbia University.

I have known Helen for nearly fifty-five years and our friendship has been marvellous.

Alexandre Rothen
Vaud, Switzerland

Dear Puddin,

"I am just delighted that the ACMP News Letter was given over to the dinner in your honor. I have heard of it from several people who more fortunate than I have the talent to be listed in its gifted membership.

Everything about the party must have been unique, but most unusual of all is having such a person as yourself who has the many generous qualities which elicit from others such genuine devotion.

It is your spirit and hard work that have made it what it is and make bell-ringing sessions such an exciting experience.

All of the participants of the other evening have said THANK YOU in their many ways but the most telling is the gleam in their eyes."

My love and my thanks,
Anna

Anna Lord Strauss (dec.)

It is difficult to pick special spots in a friendship lasting 43 years. It began with a weekend of violin sonatas (10 or more) — and for Helen a lot of good tennis. It was a joy to meet an excellent violinist who not only tolerated piano but really enjoyed sonatas and was fun to play with.

As a pianist, one feels on the outer edge of chamber music, while string quartets are its heart. The visits in New York and Stockbridge gave a perfect chance for listening to many quartets seldom heard in public (when not in the midst of music involving piano). What a golden thread that was through so many years! It still warms my heart to think of it all!

One vivid incident in Stockbridge — an evening of violent thunderstorms and roaring wind and beating rain — music that had been planned had to be canceled. So Helen and I used it for reading the Hindemith Sonata Op. 11, No. 2 (in D). She never had played it and I had sightread it once. We struggled through it, outlasting the storm, thoroughly enjoying it all — quite in tune with the storm.

Dorothy Wire
Bryn Mawr, Pennsylvania

One Christmas week when we were visiting Helen in New York, Betty and I joined a group of students to practice playing Christmas carols by ringing Helen's fine set of English hand bells.

That evening we all went to Rockefeller Center and there on the sidewalk with Helen conducting gave a bell-ringing concert of carols. Soon the crowd which gathered around us joined in singing. After that we went to the Lighthouse for the Blind and a hospital and rang the bells on each floor to entertain the patients. It was one of our most gratifying Christmas holidays.

Helen Rice was so comfortable and gratifying to know and associate with. Betty and I miss our annual week-long visits with her and her innumerable friends in Stockbridge and occasionally in New York. She had a way of promoting co-operation both musically and socially regardless of one's level of age or musical competence. THERE WILL NEVER BE ANOTHER HELEN RICE!

Carl Williams
Laguna Hills, California

I met Miss Rice through an article I wrote for the Christian Science Monitor some years ago. It led to an invitation to play at her home in New York in the Fall of 1977 while I was attending a convention in New York. Lovely lady, very nice evening.

Donald Stewart
Manhattan, Kansas

This is my favorite anecdote about Helen:

One fine evening in Stockbridge we were attempting to play (?) the Enesco Octet with Jay Rosenfeld very ably leading from the first violin. Helen and I were sitting next to each other on 3rd and 4th violins. Never having heard or played the Enesco, I became hopelessly lost and looked over to Helen (who was still fiddling away!) for some direction. Without ever missing a beat (at least it appeared that way!) she said, "Don't look at me — I'm lost too!"

Betty Williams
Laguna Hills, California

Many years ago, when I had proudly joined the hallowed ranks of professional concert artists in England, my father entered my name in the register of the ACMP. Young and ambitious, I was rather indignant at being grouped with amateurs. However, my father, himself an avid chamber music violinist, thought I might one day be glad to meet enthusiastic players in different places for the sheer joy of music-making.

How right he proved when I met Helen Rice for the first time. Entering her apartment, I expected to confront a busy secretary full of information. When I left, I had an invitation to dinner and a concert the following day, and of course a date for a chamber music session. Much more than all this: I sensed the beginning of a beautiful friendship with a rare human being, who understood to make each day a worthwhile experience for herself and her many friends.

Shortly afterwards, I married Ben in the Midwest. On our return, Helen insisted on giving us a New York reception at her apartment for all our friends. We shall always remember her warmth and generosity which made it such a perfect occasion.

Helen's infinite hospitality extended even to our cat, Katrina, who spent several weeks with her in Stockbridge. When we collected Katrina, she was noticeably more civilized: the influence of one independent spirit upon another, based on love, tempered with strict house rules.

Daphne Spottiswoode-Loewendahl
Purchase, New York

Even though this took place 22 years ago when I was a young teenager, I'm still embarrassed at my sarcasm. However, if it will shed some light on Helen's incredible ability to say exactly the right thing, I would agree to submit this anecdote.

Helen used to send our family a crate of Florida Temple oranges every January. As a teenager I dreaded the arrival of these fruits because it meant nothing but oranges for fruit desserts until they were gone. And I hated oranges, so they lasted even longer because I ate so few. When I was 13 or so, my parents decided that it was my turn to write and thank Helen that year. I resisted, they persisted, and finally I wrote the letter. The first sentences stick in my mind: "Thank you for the oranges. My parents and sisters like them. I ate one too." [I blush to write this.] My parents (wisely, I think) sent the letter off. In a week I received a nice letter from Helen. It began, "I am glad you enjoyed the oranges . . ." From that day on, sarcasm made me sick, especially when it came from me. And my admiration for Helen's "therapeutic tact" grew tenfold!

It was a complete surprise to me that Helen willed me her viola. It is a beautiful instrument and of the right sonority for an amateur with a tendency towards a weak tone. Since I use it at least weekly for quartets, I believe it is getting still more use than it had from Helen (who played violin more). I think this would please Helen.

> Jane Stein Wilson
> Richmond Hill, Ontario

The first time I met Helen Rice was in 1939 when my brother John worked for her parents, Mr. and Mrs. Edwin T. Rice (Margaret). I had gone down to their home in Stockbridge to help John open the home for the summer months and to help close when the family left in the Fall. My taking over the work from my brother was in the 1942–43 season. This was not long after Mr. Rice had passed on. Mr. and Mrs. Rice were wonderful people. Mrs. Rice passed away in 1960. I worked for Helen Rice until her passing in April, 1980.

Helen Rice was a person with many interests, among them a common bond that we also shared: music, gardening, respect for all phases of life. Every year we would work in her raspberry patches, grape arbor, vegetable garden. Helen would always share these bounties with me and many other friends and neighbors.

Many well-known people would come to visit and to join in the chamber music get-togethers at her Stockbridge home.

I remember when I would work there in the mornings. Helen would introduce me to her guests. One I remember was Madame G. Baer and her niece and niece's husband who came to visit from Switzerland quite often. Mrs. Baer's niece and her husband last visited Helen in August, 1979 and all stopped briefly at my home that day. Little did I realize at the time how ill Helen was. Barely eight months later she passed on.

During the time of my employment for Helen Rice, she started the "Amateur Chamber Music Players" and it grew from 250 members to thousands internationally.

Helen also was an active member of the Berkshire Garden

Center and everyone tasted Helen Rice's fudge that helped raise money for the organization. (Here an aside by my wife, Rose: "If Michael didn't come home from the sale with the candy, it would be a terrible let-down for me.")

One memory of Helen was the time she attended a concert given by the First Methodist Church in Pittsfield at which our choir gave a performance of the "Joseph Haydn Mass." This was done by the choir, strings and organ.

It will take volumes to tell you and everyone my feelings of all the memories through the years.

Our mutual love of gardening brings to my mind a quote of Helen's mother (Margaret Rice) which was, "In the morning Helen used the station wagon for manure for her garden, and in the afternoon for her guests." This shows her vitality of life from beginning to end and her reverence of life.

Michael Pensivy
Pittsfield, Massachusetts

Miss Helen Rice makes fudge in the kitchen of her more than a century-old home on Prospect Hill
Credit Joel Librizzi

In addition to playing with Helen in New York and Stockbridge, I had a delightful day with her picking cherries. She'd climb a little ladder and was extremely proficient. There was difficulty getting her to stop, she loved it so. I also enjoyed helping Helen sell some of her wonderful fudge at the Garden Center Festival.

Gladys Friedland
New York City

I knew Helen Rice when she taught at Bryn Mawr College and played with her once. However, I knew Kitty Bowen Downs better. Both were great ladies and I consider myself lucky to have had my path cross theirs — even briefly.

Betty Hill Hendren
Wayne, Pennsylvania

We have so many memories of Helen that it is hard to know where to start: some are music-related, such as wonderful moments during quartets, Helen's face so alive and glowing, and the warmth of her knowledge and enthusiasm carrying us all along over the difficulties and uncertainties in our playing. Or the times, afterward, when we all relaxed, devouring her marvellous refreshments. Or simply the warmth of her voice, over the telephone.

There is another memory, of a summer breakfast on the porch at Stockbridge, and Helen explaining the always-slightly-opened screen door through which her "summer cat" could come and go at will, without becoming either too dependent or too isolated for the good of either of them. What a rare person she was!

I know you will have many heartfelt comments from her myriad friends, but I would like to add one other "thank you" for her wonderful kindness to our son James, a second-generation friendship. In so many ways she was his truest chamber music guide and friend, and we hope and trust that he will share those insights and that special love and warmth, in his turn, which she gave us all so generously.

Charlotte Dunham
Annapolis, Maryland

She seemed immortal to me and I cannot imagine how we can think of the ACMP, of her New York home, of beautiful Stockbridge without her being present and greeting us with her warmth, her smile, her intelligence and her musicianship. She was such an exceptional human being, beautiful to look at and gifted, and though the center of music lovers all over the world, she never showed any sign of feeling important.

Erika Bach
Bristol, England

I never called her Helen, of course, but "Miss Rice" — which was how you addressed older ladies in the days when I was growing up. In any event I always found her the warmest and most accessible of the quartet people who came to our house. I think that was part of her genius.

Ezra Bowen
Westport, Connecticut

In Stockbridge, fall of '79

Helen had the most beautiful smile I've ever known, and her gentleness of spirit was unique. I shall treasure her memory.

Robert Miller
Northampton, Mass.

I met Helen Rice through my mother, who had corresponded with her for years but had never met her (my mother once sent a Christmas card, showing our family and our cat: the presence of the cat created an instant friendship). I was a student, in New York for a ten-week special program, so my mother contacted Helen, who then invited me to a Brandenburg Concerto party. I arrived at her apartment to find it filled with musicians, chairs and stands. And Helen Rice. Apparently she liked my playing, since I was invited back several more times, to play quartets with some of her visitors. I played with a violinist from Montreal, a cellist who had driven all over Europe with his music and cello in the car trunk (he said he once met some orchestra players in Sicily while waiting for a traffic light to change; they played together the same evening!), and more.

Later on, I attended the Berkshire Music Festival at Tanglewood, where I had several chances to play with her again, at her Stockbridge home, along with some of my friends from Tanglewood. We even had mushroom soup made with the mushrooms she picked herself! I believe my parents finally met her in Stockbridge, where they were her house-guests for a few days, and of course we all stayed in touch until she died.

After I finished my schooling in 1974, the Sequoia Quartet (of which I'm the violist) began getting busier and more visible. In 1976 we won the Naumburg Chamber Music Award, and after our New York debut, Helen hosted our reception (in her apartment, of course), and we reminisced about our first meeting in that very room. Somehow her door was *always* open, and her delight in music and the musicians was wonderful to experience.

Another common bond our family shared with Helen was that we also have a set of English handbells. I never was in New York to join in, but I know she used to go bell-ringing at Christmas, with each person carrying his bells around his neck on varying lengths of ribbon (so that the ringers wouldn't hit one bell against another and damage them). The idea my parents introduced to her was that of using color-coded notes on large placards, for the bell-ringers who don't read music — whenever the leader points to (green or red or . . .) you play your note! I think that was an idea that really appealed, since it allowed everyone to be involved, and that was always Helen's way.

One last remark before I close, and that is that Helen and her "amateur" musician friends amazed many of my "professional" friends with their commitment, understanding, knowledge, and ability in playing chamber music. And we're all very lucky people to be able to play it and share it.

James Dunham
Newhall, California

Helen had two traits that were most inspiring to me and all of us as amateurs in chamber music playing. They were modesty in her attitude toward playing chamber music, which was combined somehow with a fine sense of sureness about the music she played. These attributes went hand in hand over the years with Helen and represented what I should think to be the most worthy ideal for the amateur and his aspirations. They always made playing with her a special experience in my life.

On a personal note, the times we played quartets with Helen and Ruth were the very best occasions. Do you remember the Brahms third?

When I came over to visit her several days before her death, she told me with a twinkle in her eyes that although she didn't believe in the hereafter, she had had a full and satisfying life with music and her friends — and had no regrets. Then she said, remembering our forays into the less well-known literature for quartet, quintet, sextet and octet, that we should always continue to come back to the greatest masterpieces, in particular the late Beethoven quartets.

Bertrand Jacobs, M.D.
New York City

The most vivid memory of Helen I have is when she came to play quartets with us one evening. She was always modest about playing first violin but on this occasion she introduced us to the

Novak Quartet No. 2 and I will never forget how she led us through it, with clarity and musicianship. Whenever we play this quartet I think of Helen.

Of course the occasions when she invited us to her apartment to hear recitals or play music are equally unforgettable and I will always be grateful for the warm welcome she showed me when I came to New York. At first I was a bit reluctant to be classed as an amateur after 10 years of orchestral career in England, but now I feel that through her and many other friends, it is the most privileged status one can have.

Veronica Jacobs
New York City

For some eighteen years now I have had on my bureau a snapshot taken of Helen when she, Ruth, our son David, and I went for a cruise of an hour or two on the Hudson River in my boat, *North Star.* That important event took place the day *after* the "Big Party" given for Helen by the ACMP. I had heard it said that Helen was not a good sailor, but there was not the slightest indication of that fact as we tied up at the 79th Street Boat Basin when our trip was done.

The very close friendship between Helen and Ruth provided me with literally hundreds of evenings of listening to chamber music. As so many others have testified, Helen was a lovely hostess and a wonderful spirit.

Rumsey M. McGregor
New York City

Helen wrote me while I lived in Beirut in 1964–66 and gave me the name of a friend to look up in that city. The friend and I still correspond. I was able to say thank you to Helen in person the year before she died. She still remembered writing me even though this was our first and only meeting.

Margaret Motter-Ward
Silver Spring, Maryland

I was fortunate to meet Helen in person during our contract sessions at Wolftrap as well as the open house for ACMP members held at the Hayes' home in Washington. But my main association with Helen as the "hired hand" was via telephone at the office where we were in constant contact.

When Helen called the conversations usually began with inquiries how Sam, our cat, was behaving and whether or not the pussywillows in my yard were budding. In the summer the main topic of conversation was our gardens and the amount of rainfall. When she said, "Now Lita . . .," I knew that it was time for the business at hand.

Our conversations inevitably ended with a joyful note of "just returning from," "preparing to leave for," or "expecting players at any moment," . . . and you knew that you were just an instant in her realm of activity, but always made to feel that you were of importance to her. She was not only an excellent conversationalist, but a wonderful listener — and she HEARD.

She was that once-in-a-lifetime acquaintance, a very *rare* person. I miss the expectation of her call but her spirit is most assuredly present in the continuance of the ACMP program that she devoted so much of her life to nurturing.

Lita Pascarella
Vienna, Virginia

Helen introduced Carl and me to Greenwood the summer we spent in Lenox — when Dina was three months old. That was twenty-five years ago! Since then all of our children have had the great fortune to be part of the Greenwood way of life.

That same summer, 1957, I was introduced to the Schubert two-cello quintet and to the Brahms quintets and sextets by Helen and Jay Rosenfeld. There were many evenings at Helen's house, and at the Rosenfelds' and at our rented house (which subsequently became Merrywood). We played a lot, and ate a lot, and talked a lot that marvelous summer.

During the nine summers I taught at the Cummington School of the Arts I occasionally drove down to Pittsfield or Stockbridge, and sometimes Ruth and Helen would come to play in our primitive living room, which had been a sugarhouse. I remember one particular afternoon, with Ruth and Helen and Kitty Bowen. Ruth brought us a copy of *Francis Bacon,* which Kitty autographed for us. One of the listeners was H.F.D. Kitto, the man who wrote *The Greeks* and other scholarly works. Kitty and Kitto did not know each other, and I was amused that each of these famous people whispered questions to me concerning the other.

Music was always followed by interesting talk about all sorts of things, and we never ran out of conversation — only time, of which there was never enough.

I was touched by many things which Helen did for people — and she did them simply, without fuss. She loved her garden, as does my sister-in-law, Nina, and they always had notes to compare. Helen gave us raspberry bushes from her famous raspberry patches. One day she came to Great Barrington, and in the trunk of her car was a fine Shaker rocker: she said that it was not the right size for her house, and she knew we had been hoping to find a rocker and generously and graciously presented it to us — with not the slightest pomp or circumstance. I think one of the most striking things about Helen was her ability to get people of all ages together. She loved young people and encouraged them to learn and enjoy music.

In writing all of this I realize how much influence Helen has had on my life — and how much we miss her.

Sonya Monosoff
Ithaca, New York

Letter written to Helen January 10, 1966

Dearest Helen,

"What a perfectly wonderful letter you wrote me! I have read it twice, word for word, and shall keep it.

The dinner was a never-to-be-forgotten occasion, the only "public" affair where I ever had a good time. It was so warm and cordial and everybody pleased and happy — because of music and because of YOU. . . . . ''

Love,
Kitty
Catherine Drinker Bowen (dec.)

My only visit to the States from July to November 1963 was certainly one of the highlights of my life, chiefly because of my getting to know Helen and spending two memorable weekends at her beautiful home in Stockbridge. I was happy to see her again on two of her subsequent visits to England, but always felt deprived when her busy schedule prevented her from staying longer. The journey across the Atlantic now no longer has quite the same attraction, as I doubt whether there are many people like her anywhere in the world. She represented gracious living at its best, without a trace of snobbery, but how she must have hated some of the manifestations of this graceless, materialistic age!

For me, she will always represent America at its very best, and I shall always gratefully remember her warmth and her generous hospitality. The world is a much poorer place without her.

Alfred Russell
London, England

Brandenburgs at 15 West 67th Street

What I remember most about Helen were the wonderful evenings of music at West 67th, playing Brandenburgs "just for fun" and for the joy of making music together. Not only was she a truly caring person on a one-to-one basis but she had the unique ability to make each person feel at home in the larger setting. Her legacy will surely live on through many generations to come.

Louise McGregor Griggs
Hanover, New Hampshire

I think of Helen walking among her chamber music colleagues urging them in the most persuasive way to performance of works for the immediate pleasure of all participating but also to delight her friends. I hear her gentle, serene voice, and attractive direct manner and see her clear, purposeful eyes. But above all, I remember her gallantry in the face of death, the lovely warming gesture of allowing a reception in her apartment just a few weeks before she died (following the Kneisel Hall Scholarship Benefit Concert) and the touching fact that, although she did not have the strength to attend the concert, she stood in her living room to receive her guests with incredible grace and sweetness.

I also recall with what thoughtful concern she offered Carl and his colleagues of the American String Quartet the opportunity to run through a recital program before performing at the Pierpont Morgan Library.

Helen will always remain for me one of the great figures of the music world radiating what is truly meant by a civilizing influence.

Anne Rosen Stern
New York City

Everyone remembers her with her fiddle or viola under her chin, but my favorite image of Helen is Helen in her garden — dressed in an old flowered cotton bathing suit, a big hat, and black galoshes. I can hear her voice in my head — that low, perfectly modulated, so pleasant voice. Hellmut still imitates her crisp way of saying thank you — *"Thank* you!"' I remember her infinite generosity of heart and respect for others — (not that she couldn't be strict!) Has anyone ever given so much to so many? So much music, so many friendships, so many happy mealtimes, so many connections that came through her. She loved to tell me about the terrible bicycle battle between her family and mine which raged in the streets of Stockbridge and the pages of the Berkshire Eagle and even got into the national press. (I fear her family was on the side of democracy, and my family was riding bicycles on the sidewalks!) I remember the pounds and pounds of candy she made every year for the Harvest Festival at the Garden Center — all sold out in the first hours to customers from earlier years who knew what to go for. I also remember most vividly the last time we saw her — about two weeks before she died — she was absolutely as always, up and about, brisk and concerned for others

— in this case ourselves because we had been stuck in traffic for an hour. She had a young Swiss cellist staying with her ("I just *couldn't* disappoint him — we planned it so long ago") and he played for us — a Bach suite; and she was having a dinner party and musical evening for the children of old friends, themselves old friends. She said she wasn't going to bother with the treatments she might have had; I told her very quickly that her friend, my step-grandmother Gabriella Sedgwick, had decided she wouldn't have any treatments either, that she would just let things take their course. She was pleased, I think, that I told her that.

We rushed away to the opera, and the next time I called she was too ill to speak. I feel her life was a great blessing to all of us who knew her, so my main thought about Helen is one of thanksgiving for her life.

Alice Sedgwick Wohl
Stockbridge, Massachusetts

Helen always encouraged me and made me feel that I could see through the dazzling film of professional hardness into the realm of imagination — where we amateur chamber music players really get our inspiration — and what a nervy state of mind that is!

Cecilia D. Saltonstall
Stratham, New Hampshire

Our family always referred to Helen as "Puddin" (dating I suppose from Bryn Mawr). I never heard her called Helen by my Strauss girls Kay and Anna in fifty years. Kay was very fond of her staunch 1923 classmate. No one of us was really musical, but we joyfully rang bells with Puddin at Christmas, either in her studio apartment on the west side, or in early days on Fifth Avenue around Rockefeller Center. At first I was given high G which only came in once in "Silent Night." We would end up in a near-by Childs restaurant where we rang a few numbers and received free hot chocolates. The apex of my career as a bell ringer with Puddin was a performance at the Cos Club where I was entrusted with middle C (I was deemed by Puddin to be reliable by that time). We practiced and practiced, and so far as I remember, made no mistakes at all. Hurrah!

My Strauss girls Kay and Anna were invited by Puddin to play on a kind of scrub basketball team, consisting of Puddin, Eleanor Goss (our tall center), Kay, Anna, and a fifth whom I cannot recollect. They played on one occasion a team of nurses. The nurses did not realize what a powerhouse they were about to encounter and were beaten, but had brought several admiring fans along. One of the fans, however, had a peculiarly shrill and nasal voice and kept urging her friend on with the slogan "Stick with it, A-da, stick with it." Kay returned from this contest with this beautiful slogan and it became a sort of family joke. Whenever things got a little tough we would say in a high nasal tone "stick with it A-da!" Just why this should be, I cannot explain; but it lasted for years.

And of course, we all played tennis with Puddin. Dog-gone-it, she always got the ball back, and it was 6″ in, instead of 2 ft. out, and her lobs almost always were near the backline (just in). No wonder the dining room was filled with the silver cups she had won.

Well, what can I say? A kind, thoughtful, talented and staunch friend of my wife Kay, for 60 years. And the same for me, over fifty-five years, one of those people to whom you take an instant liking.

Harry Mali
New York City

Helen stood for something very special to me and to the young quartet players in the School for Strings. The deep and abiding love of this great quartet literature and her all-encompassing knowledge was a great inspiration to these youngsters just dipping their toes in this great musical ocean. She never missed a "chamber music party" from the time she joined our board until her death. She seemed to take an especial pleasure in hearing these very young players (some as young as eight) encountering their first Haydn or Mozart minuets. It was obvious that she was reliving some early memories of her own and could envision the deep happiness in store for these young people who could look forward to many years of quartet participation.

That she was willing to be a part of our school made us very happy. To know her has been a great privilege.

Louise Behrend
New York City

61

On the court at Greenwood

I remember Helen Rice when I was a child, especially on the tennis court, and when her father came to Cambridge on legal business, he always wore a morning suit.

It has been a long time since that summer at Greenwood on Isle La Motte. I always look back with pleasure on that summer.

John Coolidge, M.D.
Cambridge, Massachusetts

Excursions into New York for Brandenburg Evenings at Helen's were the high point of the year; it was a great thrill also when Helen and Ruth returned the compliment by coming out to Connecticut.

An even greater event was when Ruth and Helen travelled all the way to North Carolina in March 1974. We corralled about 35 players for Brandenburgs in Lili Kraus' music studio, the best place for such an event in our wholly rural mountain county.

Players came from Tennessee, North and South Carolina and Virginia to meet and play with Helen. We had a whole weekend of marvelous music-making stimulated by Helen's and Ruth's visit.

No anthology about Helen will be complete without a statement about the friendship between her and Ruth McGregor. An enormous amount of admiration and respect characterized their friendship and of course, their enjoyment was sealed by playing quartets together on a regular basis for many, many years.

Sue Coolidge Jones
Burnsville, North Carolina

The quartet corner at 15 West 67th Street

I played a Mozart quartet with Helen Rice and Ruth McGregor and Alice Mary Hayes in the home of Helen Rice in New York in November 1963 — a sympathetic meeting!

Carlos Botelho
Lisbon, Portugal

Remembering Helen's contribution to the "joy of chamber music" would take pages!

I met her at South Mountain where I was studying during the summer (1930s) and where we played in the chamber orchestra (students under Willem Willeke).

After my marriage we were in Stockbridge for the summer and Helen was kind enough to invite me to join her chamber music evenings. All ages were represented and very often were Helen's house guests. The music could be a trio or an octet, depending on the number there.

Helen's gentle encouragement made each player feel like a virtuoso so that one played as never before. She had an inner peace and a love of music, especially chamber music, that was contagious.

No doubt there are countless young people who owe their musical heritage to Helen. A very beginning amateur would be given a chance to play, somehow, with Helen and would not disappoint her.

Ingolf Dahl, composer and pianist; Einar Hansen, a first violinist in the Boston; Robert Miller, pianist, and others would join us for chamber music.

How Helen managed so much is a wonder, since she had a large vegetable garden which she cared for entirely, was an excellent tennis player and then, there was the music! Caring for the garden was not all. It meant delivering vegetables to friends and shut-ins.

She would organize a group also to do a concert for local churches. I remember that we would have but one rehearsal and it would go well, due to Helen's faith and strength. Somehow, one had to measure up to her standards, and you did!

Her knowledge of the chamber music repertoire was phenomenal so that a player who was not too accomplished would not be faced with a late Beethoven quartet or a Bartok.

Helen was full of warmth and empathy, with a love and respect for chamber music that inspired all around her. Would there were more "Helens" right now!

Bess Karrick
Washington, D.C.

The letter where Helen informed me the Board of Directors had appointed me to the ACMP Advisory Board was a big thrill and important event in my life!

Bob Maas
Sarasota, Florida

Perhaps the thing that comes first to mind is the wonderful variety of the places in which I and so many others made music with Helen: a prep school in Pennsylvania, a residence hall in Bryn Mawr, the splendid barn studio at Greenwood in Cummington, her Stockbridge home, the great studio in New York. The homes of so many friends in and out of the city, to say nothing of many industrious rehearsals in the elegance of the Cosmopolitan Club. In all these places her musical leadership and the beauty and distinction of her bearing, gave confidence to lesser players and support to many distinguished professionals.

And there was so much to study and play. The 18th and 19th century repertory we all covered very thoroughly. How happily I remember the peak of this study for me: being led through Beethoven Op. 131 and 132 with a revealing understanding on her part. But it didn't level off there. The most unencountered composition I worked on with Helen was the Florent Schmitt piano quintet. There was a time when architects were not in continual demand, and I was able to devote several intensive mornings to that mind-stretching work.

The Brandenburg evenings brought experience and joy to many people, but in one pair of those evenings, the composer was not J.S. Bach. We went through the complete violin concerti of Mozart with a soloist who specialized in those works, and it was refreshing.

One never knew who was to be playing in even the most informally organized evenings. I participated in a reading of Mozart string quintets and the first violinist was a young studio musician who enchanted us. He proved to be Broadus Erle who later founded one of the most electrifying quartets of this era, the "New Music Quartet" all too short-lived, but memorable. "Ah, did you once see Shelley plain?" Yes.

As Finnish sailors are said to be able to whistle up a fair wind, Helen could summon any combination of players together. One weekend at Stockbridge we started with string duos and trios and, with the help of the late Jay Rosenfeld, finished up with a full dress reading of the Schubert Octet. How many avocational players can look back on similar experiences with Helen's marvelous help!

The 67th Street studio was so adaptable and Helen was so adaptable in putting it to maximum use. Although most of our happy memories are of making music there, it was also a fine experience to hear distinguished recitals in such an unusually intimate concert environment. One evening Eric Friedman and Daphne Spottiswoode presented an arresting performance of the ferociously demanding Corigliano sonata for violin and piano.

It is impossible to think of the studio without thinking of the wonderful refreshments which followed the music. Sandwiches never elsewhere tasted so good; punch never tasted so irresistible.

I am only one of so very many whose affections were warmed, and whose musical experience was developed and enhanced by Helen's long, original and productive career, the career of a fine musician which was based not on ambition but on friendship.

Dick Snow
Bronxville, New York

One of my most touching memories of Helen is the recurring incident when she asked me in late March or early April, on my shopping trip if I would stop by the southern border of the lake in Central Park nearest 72 Street, to see if the spice bush was in or nearly in bloom. She loved to see the tiny blossoms and enjoy their delicate scent. We took the short walk to see them on Sunday mornings.

Flora De Lorm
Schroon Lake, New York

Helen with her 'treasure' Flora and husband at Schroon Lake

I remember Helen so vividly! She had a magic formula for combining gentleness and understanding with firmness and strength. I was a legacy to her from Virginia Apgar, who adored her, and told about marching down Fifth Avenue with Helen and others ringing hand bells at Christmas time. I don't think I met her until I spent a week playing chamber music in Stockbridge after Virginia died.

I stayed at her apartment in NYC twice when I attended conferences in New York. She treated me royally, providing string quartet players for an evening of music. She treated me as an old friend — and I her. She was most encouraging about my rather shabby cello playing. When I said I felt "naked" when the cello suddenly had a solo passage, she said, "Yes, exposed." I remember Flora, whom she called "my treasure."

Carol Bedell Thomas, M.D.
Baltimore, Maryland

Dear Helen Rice was an inspiration to me and always will be. Whenever I came to New York she would say, "Oh, how fortunate you are here! We need another viola player in the concerti grossi we're doing tonight. Please come!" Or, "You're just the person we need for viola quintets this afternoon!"

The joy of being with her always was very special. She was also very helpful in suggesting Mme. Wahl as a place for Steve to stay in Geneva when he was studying with Fournier for three years and which worked out so happily for him.

Her generosity and warmth and genuine thoughtfulness in implementing ways for helping people in music will always be a source of inspiration and a guide to all of us who have had the privilege of knowing her.

Persis and Sid Ballou
Concord, Massachusetts

I remember her unexpected help when I spent a year in Paris as a student. She sent notes to some of the chamber music players she knew that I was studying there, and they contacted me — had me to tea, sized me up and then invited me regularly for suppers and evenings of chamber music. This was truly special since French people seldom invite you to their homes for dinner — they take you out to a restaurant. I mentioned this to a young French acquaintance and he was dumbfounded.

Kay Johnson MacDonald
Reston, Virginia

Helen Rice had for me a magic flute by which she was guiding you in her world. She had that special gift to let you feel a good old friend and was interested in all that was art for you and your country. She was one of those persons whom God chose as an example for us all. The long distance that separates me from Helen's home makes me feel Helen is still alive and I shall continue to feel the spell of her "magic flute."

Viorica Voiculescu
Bucharest, Romania

As a member of the "Trio Elvetico" I was invited to the Stockbridge Chamber Music Festival in September 1976. Helen Rice, who has since her youth been connected with Switzerland, took interest in the Swiss group and invited us to have lunch at her home in Stockbridge. Since then, whenever I was in New York, I was her guest at her New York apartment, the unforgettable Central Park Studio. In March 1977 I stayed together with my wife Mei-Lee at her place; she was then helped by her friend Flora. We brought along the Swiss "Lindor" chocolates which she admitted was her great weakness. She liked them so much that she decided to hide them from every visitor and felt sinful about that. In March 1979 I gave a recital at her home with the pianist Daphne Spottiswoode, and again the following year on March 29th. This was her last concert before she died three weeks later. It was sad for all of us to see that she had to exclude herself from the audience: due to her rapidly declining health she was unable to come down and remained on the upper floor. Mrs. McGregor took care of her. If I remember well we played the G minor gamba sonata by Bach, Beethoven A major, the Fauré Elegy and the Debussy sonata. During the day I was practising the fifth Bach suite and, afraid to disturb her, I wanted to close her room door. But she

68

insisted to listen, and so I played the whole suite with the sad feeling that it was the last time I could give her joy and a little pleasure.

We all miss her: her tender warm voice, her lovable eyes, her deep kindness. Nothing with her was on the surface, everything was anchored in a rare steadiness, and she had a pure love for all things good and beautiful. I feel privileged having known her.

Markus Stocker
Zurich, Switzerland

Some years ago I spent a week in the Tanglewood area at the home of a friend who is a violist, Sam Chelimsky. He arranged a delightful evening for me to play at Helen Rice's home. She graciously allowed me to play first violin in a Haydn quartet and a Beethoven Opus 18.

Philip Blatt
Brooklyn, New York

I first met Helen in 1963 when I began to teach at Bryn Mawr. Introducing herself as a loyal alumna of the college, a musician, and a member of the Music Committee of Smith College — the latter capacity she mentioned in order that she might have some credibility — she asked whether she might visit one of my classes. In view of her disarming attitude, I was happy to welcome her. It was fortunate for me that I did, because this was to mark the beginning of a lasting friendship.

Helen manifested such genuine interest in and love for those whom she chose as her friends that she made them feel like kings or queens. She brought out the best in people. Her circle was large, but not all-inclusive. A professional artist came to play at Helen's apartment. She found him surprisingly unmusical for a person of his stature, and unpleasant to boot. As far as I know he was never asked to reappear.

She accepted a short-term position as a warden at Bryn Mawr some years ago, so that she could subtly implant a chamber music program on campus. A minority of the faculty opposed Helen's presence on the musical scene. It was alleged that she promoted frivolity among the students, probably under the theory that an enjoyable activity ought to be sinful, or at least unintellectual.

Although Helen obviously had a taste for many kinds of music, I am not sure that opera was one of them. I was never able to persuade her to come and see one with me. In her conversations she gave the decided impression that, as far as she was concerned, the salvation of the world rests in chamber music.

Although "people came first," and Helen was always looking for ways to give them pleasure, she also was fond of cats. My big black Pacha amused her and soon became her cat-friend. The admiration was mutual. She remembered "His Highness, the ruler of the household" as long as he lived, and sent him fresh catnip from Stockbridge, which he used to devour with gusto.

One area of interest we did not have in common was clothes. She considered these things necessary for respectability and warmth, I suppose, but did not like to waste time shopping for them. Fortunately her friend Ruth McGregor (and Bunny Little) selected tasteful items for her on approval, and I believe she approved most of the time. She appreciated her friends' devotion and the successful sartorial results.

Isabelle Cazeaux
New York City

To describe the Amateur Chamber Music Players as an organization is to make an implicit criticism of all other organizations. Its founding presence is the gracious Helen Rice, of New York and Stockbridge, who has been host to enthusiastic players for fifty years and inspired them with her own unfailing devotion and hospitality. The organization she has inspired and sustained has procedures that put other organizations to shame. ACMP does not merely approve the minutes of its last meeting, but savors the minutes of every meeting; it does not merely discuss resolutions, but achieves them for each item on its agenda, and with each cadence; it does not pass motions, but performs movements; its leadership does not have to be elected, and then challenged or followed, but is a function of the requirements of each situation; membership in it comes not by application, but by practice; it does not seek consensus, but harmony. When you add that the only politics that have to be played in order to achieve priority is between two fiddlers who can compromise by exchanging seats, the reproach to other organizations appears all the greater.

John D. Montgomery, Professor at Harvard's Kennedy School of Government (first written in honor of Helen in 1965).

Cambridge, Massachusetts

This is about Helen's love for young people.

I first met her in the summer of 1938, I believe, while living in Lenox after my years at Juilliard. She invited me to play several times, including one whole weekend, which I was delighted to do, but the charming part was that she insisted on paying me as a professional. Which I was, but a very out-of-work one, and she struck the most delicate balance between the social and "professional" aspects of our association.

Much later she took an interest in my cellist son Tim, and followed his student and professional career. She could name his teachers, awards, and jobs (with dates!) as if she were a relative with only one youngster to follow. But it was not an isolated feat. I heard her repeat it with several others. Of course this shows the mechanical phenomenon of a memory for people, but much more, the deep interest that drives one to *use* the memory.

Norman Butler
Washington, D.C.

It was a lucky day for me when I first met Helen Rice in Bryn Mawr. Helen was rounding up chamber music players at a community center and I went out from Philadelphia to participate. It was the beginning of a lifelong friendship.

When I came to New York I was a frequent visitor at 15 West 67 Street, playing at both "big" and "small" evenings.

When Helen decided to give up teaching because she was snowed under with ACMP business, I was greatly honored to be her successor at the Brearley School.

Aside from the warmth and pleasure of her friendship, many interesting and memorable experiences resulted from my long association with Helen.

Ann Purcell
New York City

I had first met Helen Rice about 12 years ago, having been brought to her house by Dr. Virginia Apgar. A couple of years thereafter, I received a phone call from a Swiss ACMP member, a violist with whom I had played on two separate occasions, in Zurich.

"Listen," he said, "You owe me a dinner and some music. I will let you buy me dinner tomorrow night. As for music, I've been invited to play at Helen Rice's and I told her I would probably have you along. She will be pleased to play some viola quintets."

Needless to say, I was glad to hear from him and even more so by the prospect of playing at Helen's. I've forgotten who the other two players were that evening, but they were fine musicians. My Swiss friend had to rise early the following morning, so we limited ourselves to two works, Mozart's viola quintets, K 515 and 516. After the music, we sat at table for coffee and sandwiches.

"Helen," I said, "recently I had the pleasure of playing with a Yugoslavian colleague, Maria Macek of Zagreb. It was a delightful session. We also played viola quintets. I was particularly impressed with the playing of her niece; I was not surprised when I learned that young woman was a member of the I Musici of Zagreb. Madam Macek told me that you had played at her home a scant year earlier. She said some nice things about you."

Helen smiled broadly and told us that she fondly remembered her Zagreb visit. Almost without our noticing it, she had rapidly written on a sheet of paper which she passed over to me, saying, "I have written a few lines to Madam Macek. I think you might want to send her your greetings. I've left some room for you on this sheet." To my total surprise, she had written in faultless German, telling Macek that we had reminisced about the warm hospitality she had extended to two American visitors. I gratefully added a few comments, my German in crude contrast to Helen's.

Charles Fuchs
Harrington Park, New Jersey

Helen was one of the warmest people I have ever met. She took the trouble to track me down when I left India to come to the USA, invited me, fed me, talked as if we were old friends and remembered who had played with me in India! Such treatment is a rarity in NYC. The few musical occasions at her apartment

72

I was able to attend were meetings of people joined by her warmth and organization and caring. I am only sorry I became so preoccupied with personal matters (and education) I never returned her hospitality.

Elizabeth Bharucha
Teaneck, New Jersey

In May 1972, it was our great good fortune to have Helen stay with us in our home in the country in Herefordshire for a few days. We had stayed with her in Stockbridge, so knew that she was a country woman at heart and she at once became involved in our simple life, revolving around house and garden and village activities, contributing much by her interest and knowledge.

I have never known a more competent or carefree traveler. She had crossed the Atlantic with warm clothes, a very light suitcase, her stick and her violin, even dispensing with a handbag ("pocketbook"), so that she could carry everything herself, if necessary. We are not musicians, so there were no trios or quartets here, but we have the happiest memories of her visit, with much good chat and talks about Europe and the USA. Reluctantly, we saw her onto the train for London where she was to spend a few days with musical friends, owner of a barn where they intended to make music all day and all night, so I hope she made up for lost (musical) time with them. After that she was going to Switzerland to spend a special anniversary with an old friend.

This, I think, was her last visit to Europe and we were only so sad that she was never able to return to us.

Of course she loved our cat!

Margaret Bowden
Hereford, England

Many people knew Helen as a violinist and chamber music lover. Perhaps not so many knew her as an outstanding tennis player. I have watched her play as a spectator and opponent; she played excellent tennis, and she was a great and complimenting lady on the tennis court as everywhere else. Once I watched a game she played against a good male opponent. He sent the ball to the very end-corner of the court (inside), she yelled "beautiful," ran for it, got there in time and hit it back, placing it so unexpecting to him that *he* could not get to it! (I did not hear him say "beautiful" — but I said it.)

Werner Lywen
Fresno, California

I had the pleasure once of meeting Helen Rice and of participating in a chamber music evening at her New York home. I had called her to ask about ACMP and was promptly invited to join in the evening session.

Thomas H. Reid
Seattle, Washington

Although we have always lived in the N.Y. area, I met Helen Rice only once about three years ago, and then through some people with whom we had played chamber music in New Zealand — a commentary on the far-flung network she had fostered. When these people arrived in N.Y.C. they found that their hotel had overbooked and they had nowhere to stay. Helen invited them to stay with her, though they had never met. I went to pick them up a few days later and when I came to the apartment door at 10 a.m. I heard the sounds of Haydn string quartet. Helen was playing with the New Zealand family — she and Joy Rothbaum doing the violin parts; Peter Rothbaum, the viola; and eleven-year-old Martin, a beginning student, carrying on with the cello part.

George Greenberg
Mamaroneck, New York

I only met this great lady once, and communicated several times about some music in my library of which she wanted copies, but I think I shall always remember her. She was a rare blend of warmth and style.

Allen C. Smith
Holyoke, Massachusetts

In the living room at Stockbridge

If all the human beings in the world were exactly like Helen Rice there would be no problems. Russia too would melt. Her gentleness, complete lack of guile, kindness as well as humor and a wonderful directness, made her one of the rarest people I have ever known. I knew that through "doings" at the Cos Club for 30 years, but it was more recently, having seen her more often, that I really felt the warmth of her friendship. Her tranquillity of spirit added to a zest for life are things I hope to carry with me always.

Louisa Harris
New York City

In 1950, when I was working on my doctoral dissertation, *Development of Chamber Music Performance in the United States* at Teachers College, Columbia University, Helen was most gracious in granting me an interview and was very helpful with the section on the role of amateur activities in further developing chamber music performance in the United States.

Edith Sagul
New York City

I first got a picture of Helen from my father's enthusiastic reporting of plans for forming what became the Amateur Chamber Music Players. As I recall, Mr. Strauss and my father were the enthusiasts who thought it up. With the ACMP in operation, my father's fiddle went regularly on every trip, business or otherwise. Sometimes the playing sessions included me as appreciative audience. Thus I got "in on" some wonderful music, at Helen's, at the Drinkers' near Philadelphia, at Chatauqua and at our house when members came to town, to name a few.

In 1945 I got a job in Connecticut and was lucky enough to stay at Anna Lord Strauss' farm at Hattertown, she being in Washington as League of Women Voters National President, except for holidays. When my father heard of this arrangement, he wrote Helen to ask if she had ever heard of Anna and what did she think of his daughter's living there. Since Helen and Anna were lifelong friends, this tickled Helen and one of her pet stories was of having had my father's letter.

Thereafter it became a tradition for Helen to come to Anna's for Thanksgiving weekend to work, talk, and provide the bells and lead in handbell ringing. Helping to prepare dinner was part of the program and Helen insisted that peeling the onions was her job, no matter how copious the tears. Since we often had upwards of forty or more, there were an awful lot of onions. Helen scorned any such notions as holding them under running water or any other such "aids," nor did she welcome help; she just peeled and wept. Since dinner preparation usually meant all three of us sitting around the kitchen table working and talking, I suspect this working and talking was a key factor in Helen's decision.

After dinner, handbell ringing was traditional. It was looked forward to by all ages. As you know, Helen could take the greenest of music readers and point out on the page which note meant *"you"* and then point at the individual just in time for the bell to come in. After three or four times, it often sounded quite well and we could get to "interpretation." Of course everybody had a grand time, sometimes returning Friday, Saturday or Sunday of the weekend, when we had smaller sessions . . .

Between bellringings Helen always pruned our raspberries and raked mountains of leaves thereon for mulch. Despite this TLC *her* raspberries were twice the size of ours even though we put in very special plants. She never could find enough convincing reasons for this, but she always tried.

Since Helen could route her trips between New York and Stockbridge via Hattertown she'd stop over from time to time.

If from Stockbridge, she arrived laden with fruits (including raspberries) and vegetables from her wonderful garden. If enroute from New York, kitchen "goodies" made by her "Treasure" would appear and delight us for some time thereafter.

Memories of music and hospitality chez Helen are vivid but it was the ongoing and more frequent visits at Hattertown, an association of more than thirty years that stands out as a rich and treasured part of my life.

Emily Kimball
Southbury, Connecticut

View from the Stockbridge porch

I had the privilege of staying with Helen on two occasions, in Stockbridge and later with Audrey, my wife, in New York. Helen quickly discerned, at our first meeting, my reluctance to "wash-up" after meals and my equal reluctance to play repeats!

Arthur S. Dearden
Athens, Georgia

Three remembrances come clearly to mind.

A wonderful walk with Helen up to Upper Goose Pond. She knew the people who owned most of the land, and she was interested in Upper Goose. I would send her clippings from the Berkshire Eagle about it. Upper Goose was bought by the state and will retain the wilderness character that Helen realized made the spot so unique.

Our first-born had her first outing in a basket at one of Helen's New York Brandenburg evenings. Helen welcomed all generations.

Helen's kindness came to the fore one miserable damp and rainy day when she was driving home one Fall evening in the Berkshires. A pitiful, bedraggled, long-haired, grubby-looking young man was hitchhiking alongside the road. Helen had never picked up a hitchhiker, but her heart went out to this young man, and so she stopped. The hitchhiker was our son Alex and she brought him all the way to our home. She never forgot it, nor has he.

Ann Emerson
Philadelphia, Pennsylvania
and
Tyringham, Massachusetts

Helen was dying of cancer. She was too ill to see anyone but nurses and doctors and Ruth McGregor. But she wrote me a letter. She thought it might be helpful to me (who owns an art gallery) and a pleasure to me to see a rare and never exhibited group of portraits by Norman Rockwell. She said that Mrs. Norman Rockwell was a close, old friend and that she was writing her suggesting that she invite me to visit her for a weekend in Stockbridge so that I could see this collection and we might have the mutual pleasure of knowing each other. She thought of this and she did this although she knew she was to die a few days later.

Mrs. Rockwell did invite me to spend a weekend and I went. And out of this time together sprang my knowledge of the sculpture of Peter Rockwell, Norman's son, whose beautiful garden fountain caught my attention as Mrs. Rockwell gave me tea in her garden. Out of that meeting sprang a contract Peter and I signed for a show in New York which was given last year when Peter brought over from Rome, thirty pieces of sculpture. The show was enormously successful.

And so over and over again Helen's warm, generous, far-seeing spirit goes on, creating a more beautiful world for all who knew her and for many who did not know her but whom she touched through others.

Betty Bartholet
New York City

To know Helen was an immeasurable privilege and pleasure. Her broad humanity and readiness ever to give of herself to those whose lives touched hers; her extraordinary harmonizing of her devotion to people, music, and nature were a rare and triumphant example of the art of living. Her directness and her whole being seemed rooted in a simple stoic grandeur.

Nigel Coxe
Amherst, Mass.

Was I not lucky to move, without knowing her, into "Helen's building?'' (15 West 67th St.) For such it became when, after her mother's death, she was the only original inhabitant, going back to the construction in 1902. The latest tenants, less artistic and more heterogeneous than the first settlers, even if unnoticed by her, were aware of her chatelaine's position.

Because she was responsive to the name of Bryn Mawr she admitted me, if not to intimacy, to almost twenty years of kindness. Soft-spoken, warm welcomes, bell-ringing, concert tickets, precious evenings of music in good company under her roof, meals, with Flora, in her kitchen, acquaintance with some of her many friends, tolerance of my musical illiteracy, a key attached to a piece of pink wool in return for watering the array of plants brought down from Stockbridge every Fall and, finally, witness to the last month, in which she gave her crowning performance — all these are unforgettable privileges whose memory lights up the empty place which she left at 15 West 67.

Frances Lanza
New York City

We certainly treasure our recollections of Helen Rice. Owing to the functions which Rameau's bicentenary involved, it was our luck to meet Helen Rice in 1964. Bryn Mawr happened to crop

79

up in the conversation and my wife showed her the Lycée named after Marcelle Pardé, who had served at its head before being transported to Ravensbrück as late as August '44 and dying there some five or six months after. Long before, she had spent ten very happy years at Bryn Mawr where I seem to remember that Helen Rice had been taught by her. On her second visit to Dijon in the Fall of 1966, Helen had a fiddle with her, a glorious instrument which she gloriously played. For some reason I didn't have the usual standbys with me, so we played neither Mozart nor Beethoven, nor Franck, nor Schumann. Just Grieg, I think and the slow movement of a cello sonata by Lalo which Helen was sight-reading. Most easy for her, of course, but the quality of her tone, its emotional intensity were such that I couldn't help expressing my admiration along with the privilege enjoyed. Helen Rice just said, "I was very lucky because my parents gave me the best teachers." It all sounded "that" simple. She had been fortunate and was thankful to others, completely disregarding her own outstanding talent, her work and practice, let alone the riches of her soul. This was no case of belittling oneself, but sheer modesty. You couldn't but accept this as perfectly natural until you suddenly wondered how she could be so unassuming.

We never visited Helen Rice in New York as we hadn't yet made her acquaintance last time we were over there. But a wonderful welcome she gave to Annie, our elder daughter on her way back from L.A. and lots of thrilling experiences when she supposedly chaperoned her sister. Annie often tried to describe a superb room — if "room" is the proper word — and a delightful practice of bellringing, quite a novel experience to her. That was her first trip to the U.S. So being full of "insatiable curiosity" she was out to investigate — even Central Park in the evening. Miss Rice hadn't recommended the scope or the time of the expedition, but it all worked out very well, NYC being still so safe in those days.

Marcel Jorré
Dijon, France

How I admired her knowledge of music! I always told her that she was better than any music encyclopaedia or music score, as she knew every note of each part in any chamber music I ever played with her. So I always found playing with her a very rewarding experience.

She was a person with beautiful simplicity in such a noble

way. Her calm and gracious manner made one always happy and at ease to be with. I treasure every moment of those times.

Here are two quotes which come to my mind when I think of Helen.

Whatsoever things are true, whatsoever things are honest, whatsoever things are pure, whatsoever things are lovely, whatsoever things are of good report, if there be any virtue and if there be any praise, think on these things.''

Philippians 4:8

"A thing of beauty is a joy forever;
Its loveliness increases; it will never
Pass into nothingness; but still will keep
A bower quiet for us and a sleep
Full of sweet dreams and health and quiet breathing.''
     "Endymion"   John Keats

Helen was such a person and had all of the above beautiful qualities. I thank God I was one of the privileged persons to know her.

Mary Blankstein
Forest Hills, New York

It has been hard for me to read the ACMP Newsletter about Helen and especially so to look at the photos. How much of what people have been is etched into the contours by later life and how beautiful she was.

Leora Shaw
Delmar, New York

My late wife, Lucille Wallace, was extremely fond of Helen; and in earlier years they played a lot of chamber music together, both in the U.S. and in Austria. Although I came on the scene rather later, Lucille often talked about these idyllic times she spent with someone she admired so greatly.

Personally, I was always touched by the regularity with which Helen came to my New York concerts on my irregular visits to the USA; and although I would never allow myself to expect or count on such moving musical loyalty, in the back of my mind, when I came to Carnegie for some concerts with the New York Philharmonic last December, was a little genuine emptiness when she did not appear.

I did not know Helen well, being but a husband of one of her oldest friends, but I think it was impossible to know her at all without having a very great sense of her superior but humble, and lovable qualities.

Sir Clifford Curzon (dec.)

During my many meetings — all happy — with Helen, I have tried to find something which might interest others, and found very little, with perhaps one exception.

During a conversation, the name of Bryn Mawr College came up, and from there we discovered that Helen was there as a student (about the time 1923–24), while I came there once in two weeks for piano lessons with Horace Alwyn. It is entirely possible that Helen and I may have passed each other on the campus many times.

During our travels, people all over who played chamber music with me were always glad to speak of Helen and her delight in music and people — from Switzerland, Australia, France, New Zealand, Germany, Hawaii, etc.

We felt enormous pride in knowing Helen, and with her death, we are *all* the losers.

Doris Berenblum
Rehovot, Israel

I knew Helen Rice only through the Rosenfeld family in Pittsfield who were close friends of hers and with whose family chamber music group Helen often played when I was there. I recall her eager, accurate, often inspirational way of playing her violin. She was a witty lady, I recall.

Douglas Buchanan, M.D.
North Andover, Massachusetts

I met Helen a few weeks after my arrival in the United States through my shipmate and subsequent dear friend Paul Nettl. It was in November 1939, at the home of her parents at legendary 15 West 67th Street. It was a small tea party, including Helen and Sidney Biden and John Barbirolli, still director of the New York

Philharmonic. Also present was a remarkable character, Hans Hermann Wetzler, whose name was familiar to me through the fact that he had once had his own orchestra in New York, with which Richard Strauss had conducted the notorious world premiere of *Sinfonia Domestica* at Wanamakers in the early 1900's.

Since then, the American-born Wetzler had become identified with Germany, his merits within New York musical life largely either forgotten or ridiculed. I felt enormous compassion for the little old man, bent under the weight of his monstrous briefcase loaded with unperformed compositions which, to me, seemed a lot more craftsmanlike than some of the fashionable serialist pretense rampant in New York at that time! Alas, there was little I could do to help him!

From the start, I took a strong liking to Helen — in fact to both Helens, Rice and Biden — and never stopped marveling at that Paganinian profile with those outdoorsy, crinkly eyes. Helen was in a very real sense my gateway to America, my contacts at first being limited largely to ex-Europeans, i.e., my aunt and uncle, plus the Toscanini-clan and other Europeans. My desperate attempt to "talk American" brought me an ever-so-gentle reminder from Helen that Americans didn't necessarily have to say "Amurric'n," but that it was legitimate to say, well, "American," indeed, that my educated accent was an asset rather than a hindrance in my trade! Ever since then, for 42 years, I have said "American," and not even Texas has made me change!

One of many items which established a close contact between the Rices and me was my personal acquaintance with the world of chamber music, our early involvement with the Krolls and others among Helen's friends. The invitation to lead the Brandenburgs at 15 West 67th was an unforgettable honor for me. Needless to say, any visit there was a treat of some kind, even without music, as was any visit to Stockbridge. Helen took me to Tanglewood in the first Boston Symphony season, and there I met Koussy, Copland, and Roy Harris. Also my old friend Herbert Graf, who had just started an opera-workshop there. He was shortly to produce "The Merry Wives of Windsor" with a promising young tenor called Mario Lanza. Little did I suspect that, almost twenty years later, I'd be working on Lanza's last picture, "Serenade" at Warner Bros. in Burbank!

The years passed. Still, we exploited every opportunity to reestablish our contact with Helen, an ever-gushing source of inspiration, good cheer, music, and optimism, despite evidence of deteriorating health. The year before she died, my wife and I were privileged to stay overnight at the old mansion in Stockbridge with its innumerable sleeping opportunities, indulging in orgies of nostalgia in the company of the Krolls.

I never belonged to ACMP, not being a chamber music player myself. But I kept abreast of its development and, while musical director of the Voice of America in the early 50's, did several interviews with Helen which were beamed to distant parts of the planet. To this day, membership lists contain the names of a number of people I enrolled for ACMP, to their satisfaction and lasting enrichment.

Walter Ducloux
Austin, Texas

It is simply her gloriously benign presence that I will miss, and prize as a memory. How wonderful to have known Helen.

Ted Rex
Berkeley, California

I was Helen's "resident cellist" when I lived in the Berkshires from 1950–1959, which means that I not only played with her frequently on a planned basis but also many, many times as an emergency fill-in when she had violin/viola (etc.) visitors (usually ACMP members), but no cellist. I met dozens and dozens of her friends this way, and many are still in my circle of acquaintances.

My first knowledge of Helen and the Association came at the time of its founding (1948) from Jerome Rosenberg, the second violin in my regular quartet and I believe a charter member. But actually the Flanders family provided my real entree to Helen. When I announced in September of 1950 that I was moving to Pittsfield, Massachusetts, they mentioned both Helen and Jay Rosenfeld as musical contacts for me. (They had a summer place in East Chatham, New York, and knew the Berkshires intimately.)

I had the unfortunate experience of having my car burglarized hours before I left Chicago and thus I lost most of my clothes. Fortunately, however, the Flanders had mentioned that Jay Rosenfeld was a haberdasher so when I arrived in Pittsfield on a Saturday morning I immediately located his store and introduced myself. "Oh, yes, I knew you were coming," he said, pulling out from his pocket a letter he had just received from the Flanders. My immediate problem was solved: I had instant credit in his store and acquired emergency clothing to start my new job the following Monday. But clearly more important in the long run was all the music which resulted. Jay called me at my office (General Electric) the first day I was on the job, and we played quartets that very week! The group included Helen, Jay, and Jan Stocklinski who, with his wife Marjorie, were directors of the Pittsfield Community Music School. I was delighted with all of these wonderful people — both personally and musically — and it was typical of Helen's modesty that many times over the years she related (and "grumbled") how badly she played that evening and how she feared I would never play with her again. By actual count — I, too, keep a diary — she and I played together 190 times in the nine years I lived in the Berkshires. This averages out to about once per week, remembering that Helen spent only about half of each year in Stockbridge. My total playing dates for that period add up to 452, almost all of which stem from that first evening. Helen accounted for most of my summer dates when Jay was busy attending and reviewing Tanglewood events, and Jay accounted for most of my winter dates when he was more available and Helen was in New York.

Helen introduced me to Max Weiser (violinist), who operated a summer music camp for adults — first in Tyringham and later in Lenox. I was often his emergency fill-in cellist. On one occasion in the summer of 1959 I accepted his invitation and played (among other things) the Schubert Opus 99 trio with Max and a young lady named Marjorie Kellert. Marjorie and I hit it off very well and I dated her the next day — we went to Helen's for chamber music. Two years later Marjorie and I were married and now have three boys who play oboe, clarinet, and violin respectively.

Helen also introduced me to Carleen Hutchins and Frederick Saunders (1951) who were then embarking on a serious study of violin acoustics. These two met often in Stockbridge for weekends and I was privileged to be a party to their discussions and experiments. The three of us, plus John Schelleng who joined a few years later, indulged in a very active correspondence which culminated in the formation of the Catgut Acoustical Society in 1963, just before Saunders' death. This organization took hold, now numbers about 800 members, is a worldwide influence in musical acoustics, and in a very real sense can be said to have started in Helen's Stockbridge living room.

Helen's birthday was October 16 and her mother's came two

days later. They were still in Stockbridge at that time of year and usually tried to have a chamber music session as part of a low-keyed celebration. I was an eager participant on several such occasions. Twice (1952 and 1953) these were formal parties with many invited guests — largely from Mrs. Rice's generation — and this encouraged the players to plan ahead what would be played, and to rehearse somewhat. Both of these parties included Jay and Helen on violin, Eunice Wheeler on viola, and myself. The 1953 party was Mrs. Rice's 80th birthday — quite a gala occasion, and Ruth McGregor joined us for the Schubert quintet.

Helen did much to help "the young" as she described the newer generation and sometimes an adult just beginning to play. However, she would never presume that someone else shared this enthusiasm with equal depth. I occasionally joined her in a single session with "the young," but in the summer of 1957 she approached me with some hesitancy to ask if I would join her in a *series* of evenings of this sort to do some digging on Beethoven, Opus 132. I was delighted — the late Beethovens were by no means "under my belt" and I stood to gain much. The series extended to four evenings at the McIntosh home in Tyringham and "the young" were Susan (viola), and Ken and Carey (violin), probably taking turns (?).

Helen's interest in the young included the *very* young, and quite apart from music. When our boys were small, she often indulged in her favorite entertainment for such little ones — namely to feed stale bread to the fish in the Stockbridge reservoir.

I had a rather "sinister" hobby during those years in checking the ACMP Directory after playing with a visiting member at Helen's — to see whether I agreed with his/her self-appraisal. Out of many dozen examples I disagreed strongly in only two cases. Those two, who will remain nameless, were overly impressed by their abilities. I find this statistic (only two) very heartening. By and large we are realistic, honest, and thus the Directory may be used with confidence.

Helen's legacy to me are in my memories, my fingers, and my ongoing musical activities and friendships. I have two material mementos of which I am very proud.

— A beautiful set of four music stands designed and made by Robert Lloyd, and given to Marjorie and me by Helen as a wedding gift.

— Lily-of-the-valley in my Cincinnati garden taken from Helen's Stockbridge yard.

These, she enjoyed relating, were dubbed "flowers of sin" by her grandfather since her mother at the age of eight stole them from a neighbor's garden.

Robert E. Fryxell
Cincinnati, Ohio

It was Laura Rosebault, a pianist-neighbor at the Hotel des Artistes, who first took me to Helen's at a musical evening. This was while her father was still living. Later I had the privilege of playing clarinet quintets there once or twice, I believe, and I often listened when Charlotte played quartets with Helen and when Gwenn and Leslie Heller, Charlotte's two star pupils played in one or two Brandenburg Concertos. Gwenn is now in California as concert master in a musical and Leslie plays in the Met Opera orchestra.

After the music at Helen's there was always good conversation over the cheese and sandwiches and ginger ale that she graciously and generously provided.

Michael Heidelberger, M.D.
New York City

After many years of enjoying Helen's hospitality at Brandenburg evenings in New York and in summer at Stockbridge, we are all well acquainted with her generosity in planning our meetings, arranging for well matched groups, to say nothing of elaborate "Nachspiele" spent round the punchbowl with accompaniment of tuna fish sandwiches for which she and Flora were famous. In later years, however, Helen's enthusiasm would sometimes overreach her logistics. No lack of supplies, never fear! but after setting up four stands for a string quartet, she would unexpectedly get a telephone call from some ardent ACMP member who had just flown in from Buenos Aires or Zurich, and of course he too had to be included. Quintets rather than quartets. No problem. But what if on the way back from Food City, for instance, where Helen had been buying her supplies for the "Nachspiel," she happened to run into one of her best violinists, and without stopping to count noses she had said "We're having music this evening. Can you come and join us?" there might have to be some logistic juggling.

On the particular evening about which I am writing, the

originally planned quartet had swollen to the sextet consisting of three (3) violins, two violas, and one 'cello. Tchaikovsky's Souvenir de Florence was out of the question, for we should have needed two cellos, and anyhow, Helen was just as pleased, for she couldn't stand the piece. We used to make her play it at times, but this wasn't the time. So, it would be quintets after all, and Helen, after doing all the organizing and extemporizing, found herself, as hostess, in the position of graciously bowing out to accommodate her guests. She went over to the corner by the fireplace and sat down in the old Morris chair. The rest of us were embarrassed, not only at having done her out of a job, but were dismayed to think that she probably knew the work better than any of us who were about to play it. After all, she had only coached chamber groups at Bryn Mawr for many years. And sure enough, as we began to fall apart, we heard exhortations from the Morris chair in the corner: "First violin came in a bar too soon. (She wasn't even following a score.) You will do better to go back to letter D." Helen had played every part of that quintet with the exception of the 'cello, and this she knew just as well from the many times she had heard her father play it. We pulled ourselves together, and things proceeded more smoothly until I struck a rapid passage which I couldn't play in time. "Julian, don't drag! Second viola, C sharp, not C natural." For us it was a real session under expert guidance. But what an expert! The only thing she couldn't do was play all five parts simultaneously on the "quintetron." (A recent invention of P. D. Q. Bach!)

Next to chamber music many of us recall Helen's great passion for gardening. By this I do not mean a few neat pots under the kitchen window. Helen's gardening approached the proportions of agribusiness, not the landgrabbing and "development" that goes on in California, but just a love of the earth, for the benefit of her neighbors, and not least, for her players to whom she would serve her own fresh raspberries and ice cream after a strenuous evening of quar-, quin- or sextets. She was always doing something for other people.

But there was one hitch to the garden operations. She complained bitterly about the ravages of rabbits and woodchucks. Why raise green peas only to go out each morning and find them nibbled to just above the roots? So she installed an electric fence, powered by batteries, with a charge that would give a jolt to all intruders, animal or human.

Early one morning she went out to inspect her crops, and in her vegetable concentration camp discovered a whole family of rabbits enjoying an early breakfast of peas and carrots. Then she saw that the electric current had been turned off. Who "done" it? Helen swore she had left the garden with the batteries turned on. She insisted it must have been Peter Rabbit who had flipped the switch. This is Helen's explanation. I don't vouch for it, "ma se non e vero, e ben trovato." Helen was a very special person, and wasn't it perfectly natural that she would harbour special rabbits in her garden?

Julian De Gray
Warren, Connecticut

After meeting Helen . . . we seemed to become good friends almost at once. But then, we are certain that Helen had that capacity to make many, many people feel that they were rather special to her. Truly a "great lady," as the ACMP statement says.

Waldo Cohn
Oak Ridge, Tenn.

What I most cherish are memories of our evenings, often snowy and cold, when we were working on a Cos Club program under the direction of Mariana Barzun or enjoying a Brandenburg evening with Helen as leader and then afterward when everyone was as hungry as a bear, she would have that groaning board of the most delicious sandwiches and brownies accompanied by the incomparable rum punch all ready for us. I loved playing with young and old, so many of whom have probably passed on. It was one of the happiest experiences of my thirty years as a New York resident.

Clementine Tangeman
New York City

Whenever I drive through Stockbridge something turns over in me like a key in a lock.

Anne Basinger
Salisbury, Connecticut

Dear Helen —

"Our friend Bob Coleman from Pittsfield just visited us for two days. I told him how much I learned from playing chamber music with you and how much fun it was. Suddenly to be with such a marvelous violinist and her friends and to join you in playing some of the whole unlimited world of chamber music was really overwhelming and delightful. I may have been too shy, scared, or reserved to thank you then but I'm trying now.

My husband Don Evans (viola) and I (cello) have been playing in the Chicago Symphony for over twenty years now. It's great, but I miss playing quartets for fun. Don's brother Stan is a judge in California and an enthusiastic member of your Amateur Chamber Music Players. Their father, Clarence Evans, was I believe, one of the original members of the Berkshire String Quartet.

Among many wonderful memories of chamber music at your home I treasure an opportunity to play the piano quintet by Florent Schmitt. What thrilling music you provided for all of us. Many thanks to you and with love and appreciation,"

Margy Cree Evans
Winnetka, Illinois

It was "Rowdy" who introduced me to Helen's select circle in or around 1965 and what a benefit that was to me for several years thereafter. Gracious Helen made me feel at home immediately although the only person I knew there was Mariana Lowell Barzun. Not of A-1 caliber on the violin, Helen placed me next to Mariana who was strong enough to carry both of us, and that is generally where I remained at rehearsals for Cos Club concerts.

No sooner had we finished one composition before Helen had another propped up on the stand, such was her devotion to music. Two hours or so later when our interest began to wane Helen would announce a rest with food in the adjacent dining room and the rest of the evening was spent in renewing acquaintances.

We finally said "good-night," only to hear Helen's parting words — "See you next time — don't forget!"

Otto Teegen (dec.)

Helen always took the time to answer my letters about my European experiences as if they were quite out of the ordinary letters. I am sure she made everyone feel like a personal friend.

Betty Abetti
Schenectady, New York

From a letter to Helen in March of 1980

"You seemed to bring out the best in others. They thrived in your presence, bubbled with confidence they otherwise seldom felt. You imbued us all with courage, made work fun, and produced a glow of good feeling among your thousands of friends, because each knew you knew them. To be one of Helen Rice's friends became a bond between strangers.

"No wonder your home was always full, as people wanted to be with you. They sought to absorb some of your verve, your vitality, your graciousness, and most of all, your friendship. And finally, they learned to appreciate the hard physical work you put into each job you undertook, and into each relationship you nurtured. Hard work of the most generous kind, too, of caring about people, with patience for their shortcomings, yet ready to give constructive criticism when warranted."

Elizabeth Lowell
Cambridge, Massachusetts

Helen was a vital part of my personal and musical life. I miss visiting with her in Stockbridge, also being part of the Brandenburg evenings — and the marvelous opportunity to perform as "soloist." I miss the wonderfully crunchy cookies and punch served by Ruth.

I miss our many and varied chamber music sessions and the new insights I received from Helen.

I miss the delightful stories, the beautiful smiling face, her earthiness, common sense and humor.

Hannah Tennen
New York City

I knew and played with Helen Rice and Catherine Drinker Bowen many years ago when she was teaching at Bryn Mawr. I used to fill in when she needed a cellist. In fact she introduced the Schubert two-cello quintet to me — a memorable occasion!

Ethel Dorr Helling
Old Greenwich, Connecticut

A Reminiscent Conversation about Helen Rice
Taped in early April, 1982, by Dick and Marjorie McIntosh and their three children, in Boulder, Colorado.

Dick: This is Dick and Mimi McIntosh and our children, Rob, Beth, and Craig, sitting down to talk about a visit that we paid to Helen Rice in March of 1980 when the children were 13, 11, and 9. I called Helen in the fall of 1979 to ask whether we might impose upon her hospitality so that we could come and visit New York from Colorado, where we live. I had been thinking of a number of things I had done and seen in New York as a child, and I thought it would be fun if my kids could do and see them too. Yet, it was going to be impossibly expensive for us to stay in New York for any period of time, and so we wondered if we could camp in Helen's apartment. Helen thought about it and was prompt with a hospitable answer, telling us to come ahead. We planned our visit during the course of the fall, got our airline tickets in advance, sent off for tickets to concerts, a play, an opera, and also tried to make contact with a few friends whom we might visit while there.

A few weeks before we were to go, my father called to say that Helen was very ill, and had gone to the hospital. He gave us her message, that regardless of whether Helen was back from the hospital we were to come anyway. Several phone calls later, after talking with Helen herself and Ruth McGregor, we decided that going was the right thing to do, in spite of the gamble that we might be an awful nuisance. It was understood that we would do as much of the shopping and cooking for Helen as we could, and that we were just going to take care of ourselves. We were going to be "camping out" in a field which happened to be Helen's apartment.

Our visit started with our arriving by cab at Helen's apartment just off Central Park West, and we trooped in, tired from the journey and glad to be in a place where we could settle in. There we found Helen looking very much herself, though clearly frail. She had set up our living circumstances so that Mimi and I had the guest room on the second floor, one of the children was to sleep in the library in a sleeping bag, another child was going to stay in a guest room, and one more under the piano. Rob, didn't you have a sleeping bag under the piano?

Rob: We had a rotating system of beds where we all took turns in the library, under the piano, and in the guest room.

Beth: I don't know, I slept behind the couch one night.

Craig: I slept behind the couch every day.

Dick: Did you like it back there?

Craig: Yes. I tried under the piano once, except all the dust fell all over me.

Dick: There was an awful lot of dust under the piano. I remember going under to set out a sleeping bag, reaching up to the piano frame, and getting my hand covered with what felt like centuries of New York dust.

Mimi: What are some of the things that we did when we were there that you guys remember?

Beth: We went to see *Oklahoma.*

Rob: Right, we walked there.

Craig: And we went through Central Park a lot.

Mimi: Do you remember walking down to *Oklahoma* and walking through Times Square?

Rob: Trying not to look as if you are looking.

Mimi: Didn't we go to a concert?

Rob: We went to see *Carmen* at Lincoln Center.

Mimi: That's one of my happiest recollections of Helen, because we had all brought our dress-up clothes which we don't wear very often. The boys had shoes that were too tight for them, pants that were too short, and Beth had her first pair of nylon stockings to wear.

Beth: And lipstick.

Mimi: And lipstick — and so it took us quite a while to get ready. And meanwhile, Helen was very concerned that it was getting so late and that we weren't going to leave on time, and she kept shooing us along and saying we really had to go now. Then when we were finally ready, she had us process past her bed so that she could admire each one of us and made suitable comments about the elegance of our finery.

Craig: I fell asleep for half of *Carmen.*

Mimi: Craig, can you describe your breakfasts with Helen?

Craig: Yeah. Every morning at about 7 she would come downstairs and we talked for about an hour until everybody else got up to eat breakfast.

Mimi: What kinds of things did you talk about?

Craig: Oh, mostly we were just chewing the fat.

Mimi: Remember when we played chamber music with you while we were there?

Craig: And I was so proud of myself because I actually played with you guys.

Mimi: That was your first chamber music, wasn't it?

Beth: No, he had played that Purcell Fantasia on one note.

Mimi: Right, but it was your first chamber music playing more than one note. We also had a bell-ringing which Helen wasn't able to play in, but she was able to conduct.

Beth: That was great.

Mimi: Who all played at the bell ringing? Ruth McGregor was there.

Rob: And Helen's young neighbors at whose house we went to dinner.

Beth: That's right, and then we slept at somebody's house one time too who were neighbors of hers.

Dick: Yes, that was different. That was the party that Helen had agreed to host for the Blue Hill Music School.

Beth: I thought it was at her apartment though.

Mimi: The reception was at her apartment, and after she found she was not going to be able to set it up herself, Ruth said that she would carry on with the food. Do you remember we all helped make sandwiches?

Beth: Yes, thousands of sandwiches.

Mimi: Thousands of sandwiches. There was a concert, then everyone came back to Helen's and Helen was there to preside. She was all dressed up in a red dress, and she was able to be downstairs greeting everyone and taking part quietly in the festivities.

Rob: I remember you spending that day making liverwurst sandwiches and ham sandwiches and cheese sandwiches and egg salad sandwiches.

Beth: I do too.

Dick: All on Pepperidge Farm bread. One of Helen's specialties. One of my earliest recollections of childhood music was going to Helen's house and having ginger ale and delicious cucumber sandwiches on Pepperidge Farm bread with the crusts cut off; that was the height of elegance.

Mimi: Rob, can you describe some of your early chamber music experiences? I think several of your first ones were with Helen in Stockbridge, weren't they?

Rob: Yeah. I guess my first exposure was not in a small group, but in a Brandenburg. I think we did either the 3rd or the 5th, I don't remember which, but I was told what we were going to play. I worked feverishly on the part for what was then my maximum tolerance of about an hour and . . .

Mimi: How old were you?

Rob: Nine or eight or something. I was able at least to plod along under the guidance of my Aunt Sue, who sort of maternally sat next to me so that I could follow what she was doing. After that there was another piece, and so I sat on the couch next to the musicians, determined to stay awake and listen. I think I made it for about five minutes before I fell asleep.

Mimi: Beth, do you remember going to Helen's house at Stockbridge to play music?

Beth: I remember that one evening when I was about seven we went to do bell ringing. We rang bells for a while and then you guys played the 6th Brandenburg, and so Craig and I retired to the car with blankets and pillows.

Dick: The bell ringing I remember is the one Helen set up for us with Kate and Janet McIntosh, and then you went up and visited foals.

Mimi: Beth, can you describe that?

Beth: Helen knew that I was a maniac on horses, and so after ringing bells and eating Pepperidge Farm Chess cookies (I remember that part too), we went up to a farm just outside of Stockbridge that raised Morgan horses. Helen knew the people who owned it, or something, and so we could just wander around. I remember very clearly one little fuzzy colt whose baby fur was just coming out. He was about as tall as I was.

Mimi: How old were you?

Beth: Young — 5? Then we went swimming.

Mimi: My chief recollection of Helen in the summer is having her come to your parents' house in Tyringham and immediately rush out to the garden with your father to compare vegetables. There was a great deal of very specialized discussion between her and your father on the merits of particular crops, on the best day for planting, and on what was the right kind of soil preparation — an amicable rivalry, I would think.

Dick: One of my childhood recollections of Helen in the summer is her giving me tennis lessons. She would come over to the court at the Palmer's house in Tyringham and would undertake to teach me better ground strokes and that sort of thing. The lessons were really an interesting combination — a lesson in how to play tennis and a lesson in how to accept defeat with reasonable grace. Helen was very good, and her manners were so fine. I remember having a lot of trouble taking my customary defeat with adequate grace. She was always very generous about how one was coming along, but the mood on the court was one of extreme politeness. Every now and then, I would make some major mistake through not knowing the right sorts of words to put together. I remember I didn't know how rude the expression, "A hole in your racket," is. At one moment in a doubles match, Helen actually missed a shot at the net and I in a friendly voice said, "Oh, you have a hole in your racket." She laughed with great good humor at my faux pas, willing to take it completely in her stride.

Rob: I remember during our visit to New York watching tennis on television with Helen. We were surrounded with her whole history of silver and pewter mugs won at tennis matches. We were watching a match between Tracy Austin and Martina Navratilova. I guess it was some of the only TV that Helen ever watched, but she really got into it. There was a lot of discussion of styles of play, and "Oh, I wish I could hit like that."

Mimi: Another thing I remember was Helen's pleasure in talking about her family, particularly within the context of that apartment and the pictures — the paintings within it. We were very much interested both in who the people portrayed in the portraits were and in who had painted them. She seemed to take considerable pleasure in talking about whoever it was — an uncle or great uncle — who was the artist; and that this was a portrait of her mother and so on. She had such a clear sense of warmth towards the family from which she had come.

Beth: And the portrait of Helen as a little girl standing in the field of flowers.

Dick: That was the one that struck me so, because I had seen that portrait for years and I had never known that it was actually Helen. It came as a real surprise to me.

Rob: That whole room was full of relics, with the paintings and the chests sprouting little bits of music when you opened them up; they were just chock full of every known quartet and things like that.

Mimi: And the piano.

Rob: And the piano, which was really such a beautiful instrument.

Mimi: What were you playing then?

Rob: A Mozart piano concerto.

Dick: I remember you were part way through learning the Mozart D minor. You had about a third of it well learned and Helen just loved to hear it. She kept commenting to people who would drop in that she was enjoying hearing Mozart concerti rippling through the house.

Rob: Yes, it was never singular, always plural.

Mimi: Another thing which I have as a more permanent souvenir of that trip results from my having commented after looking through the bookshelves on what a wonderful collection of English history books Helen had. I mentioned that someone in her family must have liked it. She said her father had been very much interested in English history and had bought these books. Among them was a nowadays very rare collection by the foremost nineteenth-century English historian named Froude, a set of volumes about the reign of Queen Elizabeth, with beautiful leather bindings. When we left, she insisted that I should take them along because she would not make use of them. So I now have an absolutely lovely first edition set of this wonderful set of volumes to use in my teaching, thanks to Helen. Dick, do you have any other childhood memories?

Dick: Working on fixing a record player. One summer when I was about 13, I was building record players at my father's house and selling them to charitable members of the family. Helen had a beautiful record player that had been assembled for her by the acoustical physicist, Pickering, but it was giving trouble at the moment, so she asked if I could come over and take a look at it. My fiddling around fixed it, although I didn't understand why. I then had lunch with

Helen and her mother who at that time was quite elderly. I had never sat in their kitchen before and had never taken a meal with those two ladies alone. I was somewhat afraid of Mrs. Rice, because she had always seemed quite formidable, but she was very hospitable and during the course of lunch, we started talking about the mechanical things in which I was interested. She obviously knew how to be a good hostess to a child, so we started talking about automobiles. This led to the fact that she had worked fixing automobiles during the war, and in turn to the fact that I didn't understand how a differential worked. She took a whole group of pieces of silverware, laid them out on the table and showed me how the pieces fit together to describe how a differential worked. I remember I was very impressed with her command of the mechanics.

Beth: I remember Helen's high amusement over our ecstasy in seeing our first cockroach.

Mimi: That's right. We don't have cockroaches in Colorado, because it is too dry. The children had all heard about East Coast cockroaches. When we actually saw one — the only cockroach of course in any of that whole apartment complex, who just happened to wander in one evening while the kids were there — the kids were thrilled.

Craig: I remember that one morning at breakfast Helen and I saw a roach, and we talked about that for half an hour.

Rob: I only knew Helen for a limited number of years, but one of the things that made the strongest impression on me was her attitude towards kids. She could be helpful in a fashion which didn't sound as if she was being patronizing. She was that way in tennis and in music; and she seemed to take such pleasure in other people's learning about and coming to enjoy the things that she enjoyed.

Dick: That really showed up the evening the kids played chamber music while we were visiting. She was going to have participated, but then didn't feel that she could. So she sat and listened, and you could see the pleasure written on her face at watching a bunch of young people playing, even though it might not have been the most startling musical experience . . .

Mimi: Well, maybe startling . . .

Dick: Maybe startling . . .

Mimi: I remember a couple of other things from that week which suggest the extent of the satisfaction she got from the

Amateur Chamber Music Players Association. One of them was her account of an experience when she was in the hospital just before we came. As I recall it, she had been being pushed down the hallway on the way for some kind of surgery by a very nice man who was whistling. Helen recognized it as a first violin part, and so she said to the young man, "Oh, I recognize that piece," or something, and he said, "Yes, my wife plays that, she's a violinist." Helen said, "Oh, so am I." Then he said, "My wife plays string quartets," and Helen said, "Oh, so do I." He said, "My wife is a member of a group called the Amateur Chamber Music Players," and Helen said, "Oh, so am I." Somewhat later during her stay, the circumstance was repeated almost verbatim with one of the doctors in the hospital. She said that one of the things which helped her keep her spirits up while she was in the hospital was this sense that the Amateur Chamber Music Players were carrying on around her no matter where she went.

I remember too that when we had gone to Germany as a family the summer before, Helen had put us in touch with a gentleman named Herr Westfall. He is someone with whom Helen had been in contact for years and who shared Helen's pleasure in organizing chamber music groups. While we were in Heidelberg, we sent Helen a postcard describing our evening of chamber music at the Westfalls' again with the children playing. While we were with her in New York, she insisted that we must be sure to all sign a postcard to Herr Westfall, telling him that we were repeating the occasion on this side of the Atlantic.

Rob: She had such a wonderful library of stories about people she had met through music and through all her different acquaintances, like — Oh, all her stories about Kreisler and Elman and different doctors and different tennis players and different professors. You really had the feeling that you knew half of the East Coast after hearing her stories.

Dick and Marjorie McIntosh
Boulder, Colorado

99

My wife, Elisabeth Tyson, Bryn Mawr, class of 1926, was a freshman when Helen was a junior or senior, I believe. Beth was not a musician herself, but when we were married in 1927 I was already an ardent chamber music player (violin–viola). When we lived in New Haven, I had sufficient opportunity to indulge my hobby, but when we moved to New York City in 1936, I lost my contacts.

Shortly afterwards Beth contacted Helen, who responded immediately with an invitation to one of her impromptu evenings at her Central Park West apartment. There I got acquainted with a German refugee cellist Heinz Placek (or Henry Platt) with whom I formed a quartet that endured from 1937 to 1963! Henry died around 1956, but after a few years with less congenial replacements, Henry's daughter, who was then about 20 and an accomplished cellist, graciously agreed to take her father's place with three men old enough to be her father. She made it possible for us to tackle the late Beethoven quartets.

Thanks to Helen I derived intense enjoyment of my music for forty years.

Needless to say, I became a member of ACMP when it was founded and I still continue to be listed.

William C. Broekhuysen
Delray Beach, Florida

We have many happy memories of Helen from the quartet sessions in her home to the house parties in Cummington, where we ate on a table made by her and ate vegetables she grew. What a versatile and wonderful person she was.

Edgar and Marguerite Schenkman
Central, South Carolina

It was my supreme good fortune to have known Helen Rice first while a Bryn Mawr College student, and as I play flute I thus had fewer chamber music experiences with her than fellow strings. She was a wonderful friend and fellow tennis player. I saw more of her on campus in that role, actually.

I am delighted but not surprised to read of Pat McPherson's decision to run a series at college. It would be just what Helen would have hoped would happen with her legacy but with characteristic tact and respect for what might be a priority need in this president's assessment, was not stipulated by H.R.

We surely miss knowing she is somewhere in the world "doing things that need to be done," don't we!

Christine W. Kehne, M.D.
Chevy Chase, Maryland

For a number of years in the 60s and 70s it was my privilege and very great pleasure to spend several days in Helen's home in Stockbridge where we had a "quartet in residence" and reveled in musical camaraderie.

My most vivid recollection of those happy times is of meals full of laughter on Helen's spacious porch and teary-eyed farewells via the Cavatina of Beethoven Op. 130 which we always played at the end.

Helen was indeed a unique and very special human being whose like we will not see again. I shall miss her as long as I live.

Denise Howorth
Falmouth Foreside, Maine

Letter from Richard Gibian written to Helen after a visit to Stockbridge 1973

"I was thinking of you, Helen, trying to understand where all this selflessness and goodness towards others originates. You know that outside of other 'prominents' you are among the best known and appreciated Americans abroad and to a great extent also here in the USA. But that is not what is moving you. It must have been some wonderful seed within you, perhaps coming from several generations, and which you have achieved to make bloom. I am deeply grateful to you."

Richard Gibian (dec.)

By the time we moved to 15 West 67th Street in '74, Helen was, of course, entrenched and pretty senior as well as gracious. We were (although of *very* advanced middle age) considered "youngsters." Crack off, Helen had me made treasurer in her place on the building's governing Board — she probably considered me honest enough on account of a mutual acquaintance: highly respectable Alice Gore King from our mutual past. We lunched with Helen and admired the doubles tennis trophies (Helen and Ma) together. Anyway, I got to be the Troubled Treasurer and Helen always held my hand (when necessary — frequently). I even got to be a noisy activist (with Helen's support) but she was just *delighted* to have me become a real thorn.

Helen seemed to me such a lady, real lady. Now, I am not unladylike myself. But Helen is a More Recognizable Lady. The Ultimately Recognizable Lady, I guess you'd have to say. It always amazed me that there were tiny bits of "un-lady" in Helen. I was delighted at the unexpected pepper in her.

I loved her acknowledgements of her imperfections to me. We talked about everyday things (imperfections); we never talked about music — would have been no use. I tried to be useful toward the end, and wish that I could have been more so. But I expect that we'll talk about it later. And introduce each other to a lot of nice people!

Nancy Creshkoff
New York City

I came into Helen's ken through chamber music and remained there, as all others did, through a shared love. But I admired Helen, throughout our years of friendship, for the unique qualities she brought to her love for chamber music. There was a warmth and an unabashed, extravagant love in her playing of chamber music that communicated themselves to her playing partners . . . In a real sense her pleasure and her quiet absorption in the played music remained as unalloyed and as fresh as they must have been when she was a young girl embarking on the wonderful aesthetic discoveries of chamber music.

Jacob Loft
Toronto, Canada

Some time in 1978 or '79, when ACMP had its catastrophe with the lost mailing lists, I wrote Helen offering volunteer hours to help with the resulting clerical work. She phoned me almost immediately and set a date when a group would be working in her apartment. "And bring your viola. We might have a chance to play a little bit.'' I arrived on schedule, to be greeted by a quartet of ladies — music on stands and instruments in hand.

Well, she said, there really didn't seem to be any clerical jobs needed just now so let's play quintets, which we did until about 6 p.m., when she asked if I couldn't join them for a little supper and then go over to Alice Tully Hall to hear the Primavera Quartet who had just won the Naumberg Award. Helen had a supply of tickets to distribute. Well — who could resist? Not I!

Lucretia Harrison
Port Washington, New York

I am only one of the many who sensed Helen's sincere warmth and kindness which she showed and expressed to everybody who was fortunate to spend time with her and share the joy and emotional experience of making music with her.

Many of us called her a 'real lady,' but there was much, much more behind her kind and ever-smiling face: a deeply rooted sensitivity, a loving respect for, and interest in, everyone who was lucky enough to come to her home in New York or Stockbridge.

George Lambert
New York City

My first recollection of Helen was from Greenwood. I had spent periods of time living with Lise and Joe Stein during college and graduate school days at Harvard and did some ferrying of musicians up to Greenwood. My first meeting with Helen was quite short since, typical of later experiences, she was being a gracious greeter of people at the same time that she had three or four other things going which had to be done within the next five or ten minutes.

During the time that I was in the Military Service after graduate school at Harvard, both wandering around the United States and in Europe, I kept in close touch with Helen by correspondence as to all of the musical experiences which unfolded through use of the ACMP. These included my cello teacher in Orléans, France, much playing around the Paris area during my US Army stay in Europe during 1959 to 1961, some plunges into the Baltic (very cold!!!) while playing with Swedish friends found through the directory and a marvelous experience with Mary

Louise Hafford who invited me graciously to play while I was at Davids Island just off New Rochelle, New York. Mary Louise greeted me at the door with a cello case handed to me, apologized for the fact that she had to go out to play somewhere else but indicated that the rest of my quartet was waiting in her living room.

Out of our correspondence, a warm relationship grew up with Helen which finally led to our getting together with her in the early 70's during a trip to Harvard Law School where I was recruiting law students. Jane, my bride then of four or five years, immediately fell in love with this pixyish New Englander and Helen was swept off her feet by a warm personality and a marvelous first violinist. We were working very closely with Helen during the time I took a sabbatical in England in 1973–74 with respect to trying to revive our listings of British players, and Jane and I also had a chance during that year to meet the head of the French equivalent of the ACMP. In my 40's, one of the great compliments on being asked on to the Board by Helen was the chance I had to represent the "younger generation." Both Helen and I kept our youth by this sort of active participatory association.

Helen always apologized for not responding more quickly to correspondence than she did but it always struck me that she responded much more quickly than I would have ever expected. One of her trademarks was that, no matter how large the paper, she always had a few more things which usually spilled over on to the back of the envelope as needed additions to the main text. Her writing was filled with swirls, whirls and exclamation marks and reflected the kind of buoyancy with which she greeted life. As warm as her heart was, it was matched by my experience as being about as cold as I have ever been in the late fall in Stockbridge with a house that was not known for heating or the entry of great sunshine. No matter, music made up for any discomfort we ever had in that house and in the institution which Helen created for all of us.

Donald R. Spuehler
Los Angeles, California

One afternoon Helen and I walked across the fields to visit a small Norman church. After leaving, we took one of my famous 'short cuts' home which involved climbing over barbed wire or going the long way round. After examining the impediment to our progress Helen said, "My hip is too stiff to climb over so I shall do the obvious thing." To the enormous interest of the watching cows and myself, she lay down and rolled under the wire.

Barbara de Winton
Hereford, England

As I remember, it was in 1941 that Alexandre Rothen, one of Helen's many friends and a colleague of mine at the Rockefeller Institute for Medical Research, felt inspired to celebrate the Christmas season with a musical soiree at his home in Irvington-on-Hudson. That's where I first met Helen, along with Ruth McGregor and Sterling Gorrill. Together we made up what we fondly called the "Irvington String Quartet." We repeated the seasonal ritual a few times, regaled by Alex and Genevieve Rothen's Swiss holiday fare, and occasionally met in between at Helen's 15 West 67th Street Haven either for more quartet playing or to participate in the legendary Brandenburg feasts.

What made these experiences so special and memorable was Helen's radiance, her enthusiasm, her musical taste, ability, and leadership. She had the singular ability to dominate by deferring, by making it appear as if her partners, not she, had led the way to some particular musical judgment. For me, Helen epitomized the happiest possible synthesis of rich, gracious American social heritage and a truly cosmopolitan cultural outlook. She had the rare gift of making each of us feel that, as we talked to her for a few minutes or longer, we were at the center of her universe. We were warmed by her interest, flattered by her recall of details, embraced by the gentility, humor, and directness of her spirit and its expressions in music or words.

R. Walter Schlesinger, M.D.
Bound Brook, New Jersey

Helen had a modesty about her music which her ability as a chamber player didn't match. She knew all the pieces and owned all the parts to be played. In assigning positions, in getting the playing under way and in keeping it going, she was able to give a participant a sense of sharing her deep satisfaction in music-making. "Noblesse oblige" was not a part of Helen's make-up.

The socializing over food and drink after the playing had the same warm atmosphere. All in all, the Brandenburgs probably never had it any better.

Alton O'Steen
Douglas, Georgia

I knew her for such a short time and not really well. But to know her at all was expanding. She seemed to love to welcome people into her life and ambience and made each of them feel especially wanted.

I rented a room in her apartment the summer before she died and came to know her better and appreciate her even more. By prearrangement, I had use of the room except when it was going to be used by someone else. The whole world seemed to be stopping off in her apartment — I'm not even sure that she knew everyone who stayed there. We all had the use of her sheets and towels (I brought my own, but wouldn't have had to) and crackers and coffee and sugar and salt. She took pleasure in our being there.

What a place! To walk into it was to step fifty years into the past. I loved its dark tranquillity, its old-fashionedness, its evocations and echoes. I wrote her letters about it.

We had much in common — music, books, ideas and certain tastes. I revered her for her quality and her fulfilling heart and feel much richer for having been even so small a part of her remarkable life.

Alice Meade
New York City

During a sojourn in Tanglewood we called to greet Helen from the Lenox Hotel. With her usual warmth and spontaneity she invited us to her home in Stockbridge. With great pride on a beautiful summer evening she showed us the lovely house built by her grandfather, adorned with the most exquisite carved wooden ornaments and surrounded by vine-covered trellis and flowers.

To complete our String Quartet she had invited a lady cellist. We sat down to play Haydn and Beethoven and finished the unforgettable evening with strawberries picked by Miss Rice herself from her garden.

The second and last time we met Helen was in New York approximately five years ago. We were on our way to Switzerland when she invited us to her delightful apartment overlooking Central Park. On arrival we were greatly surprised to be greeted by another eight or ten musicians who had come from as far away as Connecticut to play some chamber music with us, the Mexican members of the ACMP. The music stands were already in place and we managed to play some Brandenburg Concerti. We ended the evening with an exquisite buffet supper, prepared by Miss Rice. Needless to say how honored we felt!

Federico and Lotte Lehmann
Carpatos, Mexico

I was introduced to Helen at her home near Tanglewood, when I was in the Fellowship Program there, 1971 summer. Some friends and I walked in, and I was impressed by such enthusiasm of Helen and her friends. Here I was, a student at New England Conservatory, in the middle of a concentrated program at Tanglewood, and I was discovering the world of chamber music. That is when I signed up with ACMP — at her home — so that I could keep in touch with this kind of enthusiasm, as well as develop my career.

David Reffkin
San Francisco, California

One of the qualities that endeared Helen to everyone who knew her was the desire to give a helping hand to any young musician along the perilous journey of a musical career.

During the last year of Helen's life, just before her illness, she and I went to an informal musicale at the home of friends of mine, to hear a string quartet perform. They were four young talented girls, relatively inexperienced as professional performers, and they called themselves The Colorado Quartet. Helen was impressed with their ability and before the afternoon had ended, she had offered her studio apartment for a concert and reception, and a date was set.

The events which took place thereafter were swift and unforeseen. She learned that she was terminally ill and with her indomitable will, set about putting her affairs in order. I assumed that the concert-reception would be cancelled, but she would hear none of it. I remember at that time New York City was in the throes of a prolonged transportation strike and the city was immobilized.

No matter. The concert took place and it was well attended. I believe it was the last of its kind in Helen's beautiful apartment. She was too ill to come downstairs, but she listened from the balcony and her spirit radiated among all of us there.

Peggy Rector
Tyringham, Massachusetts

There is no way of adequately describing the magnitude of my debt to Helen Rice.

At age 77, living in a forward-looking retirement village, and still playing chamber music at least three times a week, it is clear that amateur chamber music is, and always will be, an integral part of my life. In great measure I attribute this to the early inspiration and to the great works of Helen and to her ACMP.

Our friendship started back in the days at Bryn Mawr. We engaged in personal correspondence even into the final year of her life. Although I saw her, and made music with her, but rarely in the later years, I always felt her presence "in the offing" — ready to help, ready to play, ready to suggest old and new pathways to joy through music.

To me she will always be just "in the offing," along with so many others of my loved ones, and hers, no longer here in person.

Bob Hilkert
Newtown, Pennsylvania

Helen had a talent for making time for kindliness, both person to person, i.e., face to face, and in writing letters or cards. Her contacts abroad, particularly in Vevey, Switzerland, Vienna and London, enriched my months in that strange, new-old world.

Helen's influence and inspiration were extraordinary. She made all of us, I suspect, feel 10 feet tall. But I am very content to walk in her shadow!

Elizabeth Breed
Palo Alto, California

So many memories of Helen cross my mind, but none is clearer than that of a beautiful summer morning at Greenwood in Cummington when Helen came by the tennis court where I was practicing my serve. After she had stood there for several moments, I asked if she had any suggestions for improvement. Only then did she come forth with two or three remarks that were the clearest, most specific, direct, and most helpful pointers I think I have ever been given on any occasion in which I have sought advice.

The clarity of her thought and the pointedness and conciseness of her speech impressed me many times, but never more than on that summer morning when I also saw a human mind shed its clear light.

Joseph Schaaf
Putney, Vermont

In Cummington, fall of '65

About Helen the musician: her first response, I suspect, would be, "But I'm just a grade B amateur. Don't waste your ink." Certainly she was a modest person and violinist. Whenever she felt another violinist was more skilled than she, she insisted on playing second violin. And she played it so well! When Helen was holding down the second position, you knew you were in for a good time.

Her choice of literature was straightforward: Haydn, Mozart, Opus 18's, and Schubert were standard fare, as were, of course, the Brahms Sextets. Brandenburgs and Handel Concerti Grossi were staples at her string orchestra parties. I can't imagine ever talking to her about her taste in literature, only because it would have seemed superfluous. When one is privileged to enjoy the opportunity of playing the masters, why waste precious time elsewhere?

Clarity was omnipresent in her playing. She knew phrasing and tempi cold. When the lead was hers, she was always clear and physically economical in appropriate gesturing. She could not abide the amateur who began habitually, "One, two, three, four . . . "

Balance was another forte, so to speak. When she played out, you listened because you knew the lead was hers. But I think she liked best just "fitting in." The quartet sounding as one seemed to be her favorite sound. She had no patience with musical egoism. She was a group musician.

Her eyes were always ready for contact with the eyes of the other players — the understood message, "Isn't this the most wonderful activity! And mind the direction of the phrase we now share . . . "

The music always came first. In her way, she was a chamber music teacher. In playing with her, I always heard the music anew. The joy of having shared music with Helen remains a sustaining privilege.

John H.M. Austin, M.D.
New York City

Among my best memories of Helen I think, are of her laughing until tears ran down her cheeks, and she laughed just as fast if the joke was on her. Don't you remember the one about a banquet speaker who said, "All women take everything personally." "I don't!" Helen blurted out to the man next to her.

110

When she told us this story on herself we all joined in her laughter, at the same time loving her all the more, if possible. It was a part of her greatness, wasn't it?

Elizabeth Payne
Boston, Massachusetts

My first meeting with Helen, probably in 1941, was at a Drinker party where we sang a small Bach Mass with about 100 people in his studio.

She made several visits to our house in London, and usually we could lay on music for her. At one of these, we managed to get a good team to play all five of the Beethoven "Posthumous" in about three days, because she said she didn't know them very well. This statement proved to be false!

On another occasion, we asked all the ACMP members listed in the Overseas list, who lived close to London, to come and meet her. It was short notice, but 30 to 40 people turned up, most of whom had never met her before. We gossiped, and played (I think) Brandenburgs and suchlike.

Probably somewhere in the 60's, she visited our Music Camp site in the country, but not at a time when any music was going on. She remembered, she said, a "comfortable bedroom, but outdoor sanitation." The latter is correct, but I think the comfort of the bedroom must have been supplied by her memory, since the buildings were essentially bare farm barns, etc.

I stayed with her several times — in fact, every time I visited the USA, at her New York apartment, which I associate with parties for sextets and concertos; here first I met Carleen Hutchins, and was impressed by the number of violas of her manufacture which were being played on that occasion.

My last visit to the USA, in 1979, was also the first and only time I stayed with her at Stockbridge (though my son Nicholas had visited there when he was a student at Harvard). I was her guest for quite a time — about three weeks in all — and besides lots of excellent music, and the visit of the ACMP directors whom I met, there was enthusiastic bell-ringing (new to me), and I remember her determination in picking the very last from her plantation of raspberries in which I was able to help her; also her collection of woodworking tools (one or two rather unusual ones) when I demanded implements with which to mend a faulty electric circuit. I was much honoured by being allowed to wash dishes, and even to do a little cooking, in her spotless kitchen. During these weeks, I was for several days on my own in New York in her apartment, following up various contacts of my own at a time when she had to be in Stockbridge. There can be few people so generous as to let a comparative stranger free to do what he liked in her family place with all its treasures!

Bernard Robinson
London, England

By the time I entered the ranks of amateur chamber music players, Helen Rice was already a legend. As I traveled around the world the inevitable question always arose: "Do you know Helen Rice? She was so helpful to me when I was in the United States."

Although I live in Philadelphia, I don't spend a great deal of time in New York, and when I go I usually return the same day. Somehow, the more I heard about Helen Rice the more determined I became that I wanted to have the privilege of knowing her. So, in 1979 I took the initiative. I spent several days in New York City over the New Year break. I wrote Helen and, it seems, by return mail she invited me for dinner and an evening of chamber music, December 29th.

I remember walking about ten blocks to her residence. It was a bitter, cold evening, and I was absolutely delighted by the warmth of her apartment and, in particular, by her personal warmth that first meeting. Walter Liebling, Connie Converse and Ruth McGregor were also amongst those present.

It didn't take me long to notice a bookcase upon which stood a number of tennis and squash trophies. It was immediately apparent that Helen, in her younger days, had been an accomplished player and competitor. Having played both intercollegiate squash and tennis and subsequently participating in intersectional and national competition myself, I could not help but respond to this knowledge with enthusiasm.

Helen graciously accommodated us with drink and then disappeared into her kitchen to turn out a lovely meal. Although we tried to lend a hand, she would have no part of it. I just couldn't get over how a person of her age was able to prepare a full dinner, play hostess, and make you feel so much at home on a first encounter. I began to experience and understand the force and radiance of her personality.

After dinner we made music, and I don't have to tell you how gracious Helen was both in her actual playing and in her accommodation of each player.

It was shortly thereafter that Helen lost her health. The rest we all know, but I marvel at the good fortune I had to know her, if only briefly. She was one of the most remarkable individuals I have ever met. Helen enriched the lives of countless numbers of chamber music players around the world. That I had the privilege of knowing her personally is something for which I will always be grateful. She was, indeed, a very special person.

Peter A. Benoliel
Wayne, Pennsylvania

A few years ago I had two days in New York City. I called Helen to say hello. "Can you come over right now? I have a quartet here." "I don't have my instrument." "Never mind. We have an extra." When I arrived, the quartet stopped and switched to quintets for my sake. It made my visit "home" to New York complete in spirit.

Lucia Woodruff
Austin, Texas

I was a senior at Bryn Mawr when Helen came there in 1938 at the urging of President Marion Park to help those of us who wanted to play chamber music. (Bryn Mawr, a Quaker college, lacked money to include chamber music in the curriculum; only Music History and Harmony were offered.) She lived in a residence hall as "warden" and organized her small groups of players to come to that hall on the afternoons they were free. She converted a bass player to cello, she inspired me to try viola (more needed than violin), she played with us encouraging us to read the easier quartets in the standard literature, and projected such warmth and pleasure in our attempts that I cannot remember even a frown — ever! What a marvelous, freely given contribution to her college's students!

Catherine Drinker Bowen, already famous, used to come one afternoon a week and once when I was there she forgot a repeat twice. She threw herself on her knees by her chair and cried,

113

"Forgive me!" Helen would invite us when her musical peers from the cities would arrive for a weekend of music. It was magic for those of us unfamiliar with this way of life.

Whenever I was in New York or Stockbridge she urged me — and family members too — with the greatest cordiality to a meal, to spend a night or two, and always there was music already arranged or ready to be.

I remember her with great love and astonishment too that such a complete treasure of a human being existed. But she was not a saint! Once a violinist who rated herself A played, and Helen said afterwards with considerable annoyance, "She's no more an A player than I am! And she just *threw away* those quarter notes at the end of the phrase!"

When she was at Bryn Mawr she had a red (Buick?) touring car and would fill it with students going to the Philadelphia Orchestra concert, or musicians and instruments off for a musical rendezvous. It was a grand sight with the top down and Helen's head of curly, already greying hair behind the wheel.

Louise Ripple
Honolulu, Hawaii

Helen's death came as a real shock to me since I didn't know she was ill. Then one day when I was in New York I called her apartment and somebody told me she had died. She always seemed so healthy that it never occurred to me that she might die so soon. But of course in a way she'll never die! I remember with great fondness the times I spent with her talking and making music.

Barbara Westphal
Newark, Delaware

I first knew Helen Rice when she was a Junior at Bryn Mawr and I came to be warden of the hall in which she was living. I soon shared admiration for her with her classmates and fellow students. We appreciated the warmth of her friendly smile and her gentle and invariable courtesy. And we applauded her prowess on the hockey field, where she played a strong defensive game, and her skill and grace on the tennis court where she was a champion.

Later, when she went back to Bryn Mawr herself as a warden

114

I saw rather more of her. She was deeply concerned about the deficiency of music in the college. She organized several chamber music groups, and encouraged the students with whom she came in contact to "think music."

Still later, I saw her occasionally in New York, in Stockbridge and at the McIntoshes in Tyringham when I was visiting them. I was not endowed to share her interest in music, but I did in gardening, and we made several exchanges of ideas and plants.

Her memory remains very vivid and clear to me, as it must to all her many friends. And it will endure for generations in the legacy she has left in love and appreciation of music, and in her warm and generous-hearted and generous-spirited friendship.

Mary Gardiner (dec.)

In 1978 during Christmas week I visited four of my six daughters who live in the New York area. Helen arranged a "holiday" piano quartet session which began at 8 P.M. and ended at 1:30 A.M. with cucumber sandwiches and tea! Where that wonderful 5½ hours went so quickly I can only speculate on.

Dorothy Johnson Taylor
Aurora, Colorado

Although our time with Helen was so brief, just a few short months, she has been for us a continuing source of gratitude and faith in the somewhat sick human race. Her letters came as a source of great joy to us and every moment we spent with her remains clear to this day. As the guiding spirit of an organization which bonded together people from all walks of life, all over the world, she contributed much more than the great joy of chamber music. Music is THE international language and when one stops to consider that ACMP is therefore able to cross the boundaries of politics and economics which divide the world, the work of Helen and all those who keep ACMP alive and well, assumes awe-inspiring importance. "Awe-inspiring" seems a strangely inept word to apply to Helen, whom we all loved as a dear friend, but Ernie and I have found that Helen, along with Lady Casey (wife of Baron Casey), and that wonderful educationist, Winifred West, have truly helped and inspired us as they must have done for so many others. If only we could return to Stockbridge and Ernie could sit down with her again to enjoy

Bach, Beethoven and Co., and I could borrow her straw hat and old trousers, again to potter among the raspberries!

Ruth and Ernest Llewellyn
Mittagong, Australia

We were both gardeners and Helen had found a place to get free horse manure. She was delighted. As we busily shoveled she remarked, "This is almost as close a bond as quartets."

She called one day, "Gertrude, I'm in terrible trouble." She had been feeding a scrawny cat which appeared, only to find there were also kittens. Since she was to leave for four days, she worried about them. Of course I offered. The beautiful kittens I put in a cage and took to the Harvest Festival. Helen was very firm about their being really wanted before she'd give them up. I kept the mother and named her Pansy because of her pretty face. Helen said sternly, "No cat who defended her babies as she did should be named Pansy," so I changed her name to Oryza which is the generic name for Rice.

Helen was honestly generous, not lavish. I had been to NYC for a weekend with friends, staying at a hotel, and was nonplussed by how much it cost me. That Fall, Helen invited me *and* my son Cy to come down during my Christmas vacation. She bought seats for four plays and wouldn't hear of repayment. I left a check on the bureau but got it back in the mail. I never tried again to repay her in money.

There was a sort of innocent greediness in her. The manure was one time. She couldn't be satisfied that she had enough. Another time we drove to Connecticut to pick strawberries. Here again she wanted more and more. Though I'm sure she gave most of them away.

She had her little vanities too. She'd had a bad cold and I suggested she wear something on her head. No. It took the curl out of her hair.

I always felt she was a Stockbridgian but once, when I remarked on "those New Yorkers" she looked at me and said sternly, "Is that what you think about New Yorkers?"

I loved to watch her make her famous punch. She was so abandoned about it. For someone who didn't drink, she sloshed the rum into the bowl and it certainly was good.

I admired her way of entertaining. She knew she wasn't "really a cook" but had developed some good recipes and was smart

The dining-porch in Stockbridge

enough to stick to those. Her sandwiches were exceptional. I found out what her secret was, but won't divulge it for publication.

A unique and beautiful and lovable person.

Gertrude Moore
Stockbridge, Massachusetts

One can hear the energetic, cheerful voice talking beside one, reflecting vitality and perpetual interest in the young. Her way into each part of conversation was by "Oh, . . .," the built-in pause of one to whom words might well have been the secondary means of communication. For surely her physical expression and her intellectual force, were those attributes that spoke first to her young friends and those to which they responded without inhibition and from their depths, with happiness and trust.

Mason took me, before we were married, to an evening of Brandenburgs at Helen Rice's house in New York. We sat with a few others just inside the archway of the other room while the players sat around what feels in memory to be a fireplace. Afterwards were refreshments and conversation, the shame of admitting that one played no instrument, and the very politeness of people to whom this state in anyone was beyond their understanding, but not beyond their compassion.

117

Watching Helen Rice stride up the hill at Greenwood, her cane in her left hand, her left leg swinging from her hip energetically, her head forward, leading her body toward the flagstones, the talk, the friends, and the benches which she herself had helped to build when the camp was begun, we felt part of her world then: our children had sat on those benches in jeans, and in the formality of white shorts. They played; her interest and pleasure were a part of a communal interest and pleasure in the elements, the phrases and the music that children and adolescents could bring forth with their friends.

There were occasional Brandenburg evenings in the summer when all five of ours could play, at least for a while. In fact, the whole family, but one, could play. As an evening went along, the youngest and then the next would come and join the spectators, for no one deigned to talk down to beginners. Each would have "a partner" and a partner could sing you in, talk you in, or point you in, but no one stopped, unless there was an enormous break in the purpose or the meaning of the music. Helen got our oldest "hooked," he was ready to be hooked, having loved with all his heart, Greenwood. She helped to find him quartets and the like in Stockbridge and Lenox where he lived for a winter between school and college. She organized one afternoon a family collection where she dubbed me the guest artist and had me play the C on my viola in a Purcell piece in which the rest of the strings play above, below, and through a continual C. " . . . and you didn't make one mistake." I was for the first time part of a string group making music.

Pleasure in the happiness and belief in the triumph of the human spirit expressed in her music and in ours — one can only remember Helen with the depths of affection and love and a persistent belief that one can do a little better this time . . . .

Peggy Harding
New York City

Something about Helen? Somebody should note her tendency to downplay and undersell herself, and what she meant to the ACMP.

On the personal level, I remember the first time I was awed by all those tennis trophies. She kept the trophies for doubles matches in the front, and when I asked, said "I had a good partner," (usually her mother). Only when I got to the back three rows and the singles trophies did she admit, and then it was something like "I had a good year or two." She made light of her woodworking abilities, even though the benches on the Greenwood porch have stood more abuse than wood was made to bear. Even her way with children — she claimed I was the only baby who never cried when she held it, but I have a picture of my Jane looking up at those crystal beads while in Helen's arms — and no tears or screams. And how she buoyed a young violist at the end of a quartet by saying how well everybody played except herself.

As for the ACMP, we all know that no other organization so numerous and widespread was created or held together so much by one person's enthusiasm, generosity, and work. Enthusiasm — her love of people and music, combining to bring people together so that any night, anybody who wanted to play was invited to her home. Generosity — her continued willingness to bear with people the rest of us wouldn't. Work — obviously, all the letters and correspondence, Newsletters that showed the ACMP had a heart and soul — hers.

They threw away the mold when they made Helen, unfortunately for all who didn't know her.

David McGregor
Forest Hills, New York

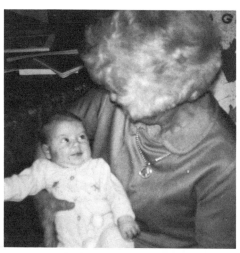

With Jane McGregor 1974

119

The Stockbridge porch with viol bodies

Helen brought our family up to chamber music. An early, memorable occasion for me was her introducing me to Bach in a small orchestra at the Brearley School. She assumed we would love it, and I did, with the spontaneous gratefulness of a 12-year-old. Then I remember a week two or three years later that she spent looking after us in the Berkshires while my parents were away, during which she also coached us in chamber music. She had a teacher's gift of listening, a teacher's patience in explaining, and her own especially courteous style of encouragement. I can hardly remember anyone who was so courteous to children. She also taught me to play tennis, and made it a permanently graceful activity in my imagination.

Not all our musical education was Edenic. There was one summer when Helen and Ruth McGregor worked for weeks and weeks with all the McIntosh children on the Beethoven Septet and on "Eine kleine Nachtmusik." This last piece has been for me, like peanut butter, an irretrievably overdone pleasure. We clearly needed discipline and we got it. But discipline was part of the excitement of learning to play with Helen. I have especially happy memories of many pieces of chamber music Helen cherished and taught us, with all her care for minute particulars: among others, the Mozart G Minor Viola Quintet, with its guttural murmurs in the Second Viola, and the Cavatina from Beethoven's Opus 130, my introduction to late Beethoven.

In later years I often stayed with Helen in her New York apartment — she would put me up if I needed to stay for a conference or whatever. It was a mark of her culture that every coming together of persons in a house was an occasion, to be carried off with style; nothing could be more cozy or pleasant than meals in her kitchen. In her manner, her voice, and her disinterested generosity of attention she stood for Old New York in my mind as much as anyone I knew, an important conception for a literature professor to experience. The apartment itself was an artist's refuge in the great city, with its paintings, its books (I'll always be thankful to Helen for her gift of the 1906 edition of Thoreau's *Complete Works,* with which I wrote my Ph.D. thesis), and its special architectural design, seemingly made for the express purpose of persuading a chamber orchestra that they belonged there. Helen's Brandenburg evenings were some of the best musical occasions New York had to offer as far as I was concerned. Yet, while she stood for a particular culture, she also took it on herself to be hostess to the whole world of amateur musicians; and though she was always very much herself as a hostess, she was passionately curious and scrupulously understanding of everyone who played chamber music with her — in her own way she was both a world citizen and an American democrat. I was touched when I saw her in England in 1972 by the great respect with which she was treated by English musicians. They clearly knew who deserved honor.

My first and last memories of Helen are images of her in the country — coming to see us in her old wooden station wagon during the war and long afterwards, at a later date, checking out the raspberry bushes with my father, and finally welcoming me and my wife in Stockbridge and taking us to a remote pond so that a Venezuelan could see New England. (A policeman stopped us on some obscure local pretext, but Helen faced him down like the old settler she was.) Her Stockbridge house aged gracefully with her, with its towering trees and shrubs, its deep-set living room for music, and its summer porch for brownies, cucumber sandwiches, and conversation. Helen was an eager listener always, on that porch and elsewhere. She never lost the gift of making me feel that I had unique ideas and information to exchange with her.

Jim McIntosh
Ann Arbor, Michigan

The Stockbridge living room

In 1964 when I first visited Helen in Stockbridge I had plenty of time to discover the library in the living room as I was not an instrument player. Being very interested in painting, I found a book on the theory of colors, entitled "Modern Chromatics," by the physicist Ogden N. Rood. Helen noticed me reading the book and told me the author was her grandfather who had taught physics at Columbia College. She added that she was told the theory developed in that book was the basis of pointillism painting in France. About two years later, I read in the Gazette de Lausanne a summary of a new book on Seurat, in which it was stated that this painter had applied to his paintings the theories of the American and French physicists Rood and Chevreul. I immediately sent the article to Helen who was very enthusiastic when she read it. She came over to Switzerland in the same year and bought several copies of that book and even tried to meet the author, Mr. A. Perruchon, but unfortunately he had died by that time. Since then Helen showed a greater interest in painting, went to exhibitions, and began to have pleasure contemplating paintings. During my second trip in 1979, we visited the Clark Collection in Williamstown and the Fine Arts Museum in Boston. The questions raised then by Helen while looking at paintings of Impressionists, mainly Monet, revealed that these works were for her something more than just "nice" pictures. This faculty I discovered in her will always be cherished in my memory.

Jean Sahli
Corseaux, Switzerland

Helen was my godmother, chosen by my mother in spite of the great distance between the two continents. I was 18 years old when Helen came over again to Europe — it was love at first sight and since the first time I met her I have always adored her. I had just started the violin — too late alas — and Helen, who loved chamber music, made me play a movement of a Haendel sonata for two violins, with my mother at the piano. What an emotional experience I went through — it was all I had hoped for without being conscious of it. It was my entering into the world of chamber music and understanding and sharing the spirit Helen put into it.

Anne-Tillie Sahli
Corseaux, Switzerland

Helen with her god-daughter, Anne-Tillie Sahli

123

My violin teacher, Samuel Gardner, organized the first Juilliard String Quartet in 1934. We played many times at the home of Helen Rice and, with other guests, had the opportunity to play a variety of the best chamber music. I remember Helen Rice as a fine musician and a gracious hostess.

Cornelia Basky Sheary
Temple Hills, Maryland

Helen had many creatures in the garden; some of them nibbled at her vegetables. First she put up a fence, but to no avail. When I suggested that she leave traps she said "I would rather see the animals alive and do without my vegetables."

She gave me my first chamber music, and encouraged me to play quartets. One evening the two of us had five handbells each and we had a friendly contest, going faster and faster. Even Papa, who was tone deaf and didn't play any instrument, was able to keep time with Helen.

Her favorite cactus plant was the "Night Blooming Cereus," and she never failed to show it to me.

Helen enjoyed cooking; her "American sandwiches" and breakfast cereals were delicious.

After a Tanglewood concert, at the exit from the grass parking lot, the muffler on her car gave out. What a noise! Helen was not at all thrown off or upset; she drove her "airplane" with aplomb. We laughed all the way home.

Isabelle Sahli
Lausanne, Switzerland

I first met Helen at a picnic she gave for the students at South Mountain, summer 1936.

She was beautiful, all brown curls, brown eyes and suntanned, busily slicing home-grown tomatoes and seeing that everyone was well nourished.

Later I played my first string quartets with Helen and a new world suddenly existed for me, thanks to her.

Marshall had met Helen in the late 1920s during his studies with Salmond at Mannes. Several years later on his return from study in Europe, he was delighted to accept Helen's invitation for Brandenburgs, Friday, January 5, 1940, as was I — ah!

There in that wonderful room full of happy people and Bach, Marshall and I met. We became Helen's first "couple," I believe.

We were fortunate in being near-neighbors. Our first apartment was at 50 West 67 Street and a house in Stockbridge was acquired because Helen was there.

I remember her wonderful smile as she would 'ease by,' station wagon laden with garden produce, music, stands, and good cheer.

Thoughtfulness for others which knew no bounds, her enjoyment of life, great knowledge and delightful humor made her very, very special to Marshall and me.

Louise Driggs
Washington, D.C.

In Stockbridge 1979

To me, Helen has always been the epitome of a great lady — gracious, considerate and eminently generous. I always felt that the shortest road to Helen's heart was through her music and very much regretted not playing an instrument. So all I could do was admire and love her from the sidelines.

Gaby Biden
New York City

I knew her as a warm, thoughtful person who had every reason to be self-important but was absolutely free from vanity or egotism. Despite being cosmopolitan with a superior intellect she had a knack for finding common ground with us. Our visits to New York City or Stockbridge generally included our children, so Helen would choose an activity to entertain them — the Empire State building, the Statue of Liberty, the Circle Line cruise around Manhattan, and a meeting with Mrs. Norman Rockwell were some of the treats she arranged.

We never did know the musical Helen, although I did ask once if she would play her violin for us. She respectfully declined and showed us how to ring handbells instead. Looking back I realize that Helen made it very easy for us by concentrating on our interests. Her modesty would have prevented her from discussing her own accomplishments. Just my fondness for her was enough reason to want to share special moments.

Serving as the family representative in closing the apartment and distributing or disposing of Helen's belongings was exceedingly traumatic and I never did get used to being in the apartment without her there.

Ted Rice
(Edwin T. Rice II)
North Stonington, Connecticut

Fifteen West 67th Street has always been the "House of Rice" to my late brother Chet and me (and our parents, too). Helen's maiden aunts lived there as well as cousins Edwin, Margaret and Helen. It was a special treat to go there for a tea or dinner and enjoy their kindness and hospitality.

Both homes were hung with William M. Jackson Rice's skillfully done portraits of various family members, landscapes and even studies of some of Cousin Margaret's prize cats. Many portraits are now to be found in numerous Rice-related households, including ours.

Whenever we could, Chet and I were pleased to accept Helen's invitations to listen to the musicians she had assembled for a particular evening of chamber music. Those participating musicians obviously derived much pleasure from their music-making (in that high ceilinged room hung with many of the above-mentioned portraits) — as we did from listening to them!

I'm not certain how long Helen did wood carving, but I do know she carved a most fitting mantel for the dining room fireplace in our house in Wilton — the place we inherited from our Uncle Nelson Spencer who, during his lifetime was devoted to Helen and her parents.

Helen was such a warmly sincere and gracious person and made us proud to know and tell people whenever we could, that she was our cousin.

For so many — surely her memory will long remain because of her fantastic devotion to the Amateur Chamber Music Players.

I know I shall always remember and miss her.

Caroline B. Rice
New York City

Helen with Ted and Polly Rice and family 1967

I remember visiting Helen several times over many years. We were invited to her beloved Stockbridge in October, for a weekend with cousins Caroline and Chester, Jean and Charlie Rice. We

127

all drove up and for the first time I saw the place I had heard so much about; Helen and her mother, Aunt Margaret, playing tennis, the music festival at Tanglewood, and the garden which produced so much. We ate delicious food, took walks, played the bells, and talked over old times. Then, at 3 A.M. we all had to get out of bed, and go to the Garden Center, named after her mother, and see the night-blooming jasmine which only blooms once every five years, ten years or such. It was very impressive.

We also played the bells in the New York apartment with the family, and my Bob often bragged about his tennis playing champion cousin who taught music at Bryn Mawr.

Helen came to Remsenburg, where she had visited as a child, one spring weekend, and Bob took her out in an open boat to see the ocean and bay, soaking her, and she didn't seem to mind a bit, only thrilled to see scenes of old.

We were also fortunate to persuade her to come and enjoy Thanksgiving with us all. She really enjoyed the grandchildren, and they, her. She seemed so well then, it was hard to find her so ill so soon afterward.

She was a very warm, many faceted person, and I wish I could have seen much more of her, because I loved her immediately. Each of our grandchildren and children has a special memory of her; she had something for each one. She was one to remember very fondly.

Sis Rice (Mrs. Robert)
Remsenburg, New York

My memories of Helen go back to the early 1930s after I married her cousin Charles. We spent a very special Sunday near the end of September up in Stockbridge.

Beside her music, the music camp, etc., she played excellent tennis and won many trophies as an amateur player in their New England championships. She trounced Charlie often, as his sport was golf.

In later years our pleasure was to go up to see how beautifully her garden was growing with all kinds of vegetables. We relished those as I am sure many others did during the summer — especially when it came to the raspberry season, too.

The last fall we went up, she drove my son Ted and his wife Polly and me over to the lovely lake which she loved and we took bread for the fish and ducks. She said she went often because

Bob and Sis Rice, Charlie, Caroline, Jean, and cousin Helen — 1969

of the beauty of the spot, and it was so restful when she was tired and wanted to relax a while.

Mrs. Charles Rice (Jean)
West Hartford, Connecticut

I believe the most impressive and exciting personal recollections during the many years I knew Helen were the following: (1) Helen's surprise party, (2) Her visit to Interlochen, and (3) A dinner at the Cosmopolitan Club in New York (she insisted upon treating), where we discussed each other's past (family and musical backgrounds) and she gave me a little blue book (more later). She was always a great delight to be with, always being intensely interested in her visitor and minimizing her own illustrious self.

(1) The surprise party was magnificent and a highlight in my life. To me she was the princess of music that evening. I loved her. I recall the night before when Ruth McGregor slipped a message to me which contained three letters from France which I was asked to read at the party. (We also had a great evening playing string quartets that evening.) What beautiful friends and what accolades! This will remain in my memory forever.

(2) Her visit to Interlochen was another memorable occasion. She seemed to illuminate the entire camp with her presence. Joe Maddy, the founder of the National Music Camp, arranged for quartets every evening in which Helen and I participated. Helen played beautifully. If she claimed she was an amateur, I would have to add, an amateur with a professional approach. A meeting of all ACMP guests was called and I had the honor to introduce this great lady as Miss ACMP.

(3) The little blue book. This book was written by her father, Edwin T. Rice, who was a fine cellist and an attorney. Many years before I ever knew there was a Helen Rice, a very good friend of mine, a law student at Harvard, told me the exciting story about the Flonzaley Quartet, in which the violist, Mr. Bailly, resigned and insisted the name of the quartet would have to be dropped since he was no longer a member. It came to trial. It was the first case of its kind in the history of legal annals. The Flonzaley Quartet won and the name remained the same. I was thrilled, because as a teenager I idolized the members of the quartet, always following them around when they were in Detroit. Many years later, Helen gave me this little blue book; a complete history of the case, written by her father who was the attorney who won that case.

Playing quartets with her in her home or apartment in New York was always a thrill and the dinners were wonderful.

A kinder, more generous lady I have never met, and she has left a tremendous void in my life.

Aaron Farbman
Grosse Pointe Park, Michigan

I had heard from Paul so much about his dear and wonderful friend, Helen Rice, but I first met her after his death when I visited her at her home in Stockbridge. I shall always be grateful for having known her. On my arrival with a heavy suitcase, and knowing I had a bad back, she seized my suitcase and carried it upstairs. I was almost in tears with anxiety, but she would not be dissuaded.

While there, a walk up to her vegetable garden and picking beans with her, gave me another facet of her character — her love of and closeness to nature and the beauty of the world we live in.

Driving into the village one morning we stopped at a red light and people called to her from all four corners, it seemed, and ran out just to have a word with her. Everyone who knew her loved her and appreciated her — knew her for the rare person that she was.

She was the "listener" of the world! I brought a friend to lunch with her one day, who had lived long in Afghanistan and knew that wonderful country and its people well. Helen listened, with every pore of her body, it seemed — spellbound. I felt myself watching her listening, more than to my friend who was talking. This quality of listening I noticed watching Sarah Bernhardt years ago not long before her death. She, too, great performer that she was, was a superb listener. What more can I say? Who that knew Helen could help loving her?

Audrey Chancellor
Philadelphia, Pennsylvania

Helen 'listening'

The quality that made Helen Rice so special was her ability to make *you* feel special. Many was the time that I called Helen to see if I could use her apartment to practice in, when the Boston Symphony was on tour in New York. After all, how many hotel guests would willingly be subjected to several hours of repetitive practice on the piccolo! Helen was always "delighted" to have me come and somehow managed to convey the impression that I was doing her the favor, instead of the other way around. As a matter of fact, I was there, practicing, the day Helen came back from the hospital with the knowledge of her own great illness. She, Ruth McGregor and I had lunch in the kitchen and Helen was her usual very gracious hostess. I remember that she said she had always wanted to lose weight, but that this was a rather bizarre way to do it. A touch of humor to make things easier for her guests.

On one occasion, before I bought my own little house in Stockbridge, my mother came to visit me in my rented cottage. But she felt bored there, with nothing specific to do, except go to concerts. She really missed her garden and having her hands in the soil. The minute I introduced Helen to Mother, she knew that the nicest thing she could do would be to invite Mother to help her in her own garden. So the two of them spent a lot of time that summer pulling weeds and chatting.

So many wonderful memories of her thoughtfulness, consideration and warmth; charming lunches on her porch in Stockbridge and in the kitchen in New York, the summer I stayed with her (my first summer as a member of the Symphony); the chamber music sessions she arranged so I could play first violin (on the flute) in Haydn Quartets.

So many remembrances of a beautiful lady.

Lois Schaefer
Jamaica Plain, Massachusetts

Helen Rice was the kind of friend one could always count on for encouragement, thoughtful and understanding, as well as straight-shooting criticism. At the pinnacle of chamber music not only as a violinist herself, but as hostess to the world of musicians, both amateur and professional, Helen carried on the family tradition of "Hausmusik" in her lovely spacious studios in both New York City and Stockbridge, Massachusetts, where she would often gather together 30 to 40 players for a "Brandenburg evening," on a few quartets, or perhaps the Enesco Octet which her father introduced to the United States.

It was this environment that nurtured the early development of the "New Violin Family" instruments, as well as my own early beginnings in violin making. When my first viola was finished, Helen really did eat her hat (made of cake and gum drops, not a dissolved-up one as my chemist husband suggested) at a party for over 50 people where SUS #1[2] was played in concert by Louise Rood with Irene Jacobi at the piano and Frederick Jacobi, the composer, turning pages of his Fantasy for Viola and Piano.

Each summer for many years during the 1950's and early 60's, Frederick Saunders' research group of four, affectionately named the "Catgut Acoustical Society," met in Helen's home in Stockbridge to discuss fiddle acoustics and play chamber music, trying out the musical effectiveness of various experimental instruments with Helen and her friends. It was here that the first trial of some of the new instruments took place in 1961, and then later in New York City, the first full scale demonstration of the whole new violin family, with such musicians present as Lillian Fuchs, William Kroll, George Finckel, Henry Brant, Sterling and Lilla Hunkins, Louise Rood, Sonya Monosoff, Irene Jacobi, Ruth McGregor, Florence Duval Smith, Rembert Wurlitzer, Henry Allen Moe, Kellum Smith, and many others.

Although the new instruments did not adapt congenially into the repertoire of classical chamber music (they were not designed to do so), Helen was most encouraging in letting us try them out in various musical contexts. One day, when I was trying to demonstrate several of them to some friends, Helen fixed me with her eye and said kindly, "Hutchie, if you really want people to like your new instruments, don't play them yourself!"

The great lady of chamber music has gone on, and the musical heritage she fostered around the world will continue to grow for a long time.

Carleen M. Hutchins
Montclair, New Jersey

Within two weeks of her death, Helen dictated to Gaby Biden various things she wanted to have remembered. The following story of Susie the Pig was one of her favorites and we reproduce excerpts from it here.

The Saga of the Pig, Susie Snowwhite

When I went to teach at the Brearley School in the Autumn of 1945, I met Carleen Hutchins at lunch the day before the students arrived. I wish I had a tape of our conversation, because when lunch was concluded, we had made an agreement that if I brought a baby pig for her laboratory, she would play viola in my students' ensemble groups. Carleen taught Science to the younger classes and in her Lab were a variety of animals — guinea pigs, fish, rabbits, a rooster, etc. In a way, it didn't seem so impossible to have a pig join them, but I admit that at first I did not take our pact too seriously.

I had learned to milk cows during the war, and I knew that there would be a litter of pigs very soon at the farm in Stockbridge. When I went up there that next weekend, there had been born 11 white as snow little piglets. The following week in New York, when I found that Carleen was indeed very serious, I asked permission of Milly McIntosh, then Head of the Brearley School, to bring a piglet to the School and she answered that, if Carleen wanted one, it was perfectly all right.

When I got back to Stockbridge the next weekend, I found that all the little piglets had doubled in size. So I knew I must make haste. I picked a charming female, bought a nursing bottle, expecting her to suck anything the way kittens and puppies do, but, not at all — when I offered her the bottle, she went into a rage and chewed the nipple all to pieces. So I had a pig on my hands that would not eat. However, I took her to the Brearley that Monday and left her in Carleen's Lab early in the morning, thinking that the responsibility was now Carleen's and not mine.

Carleen Hutchins with Susie at the Brearley School

134

To my dismay, when I went down at lunch time, I learned that Carleen and her husband had gone to Vermont for a funeral. Various people tried unsuccessfully to coach the pig to eat. Even the McIntoshes, who were then living at 87th Street, failed despite all the efforts of their young family. So the pig became my responsibility again and I finally dunked her nose in a saucepan of warm milk and she got the idea, after which she gained 17 lbs. of what my mother called: "the intellectual garbage of the Brearley School." We named her Susie Snowwhite. She was immaculate and looked as if she were walking on high white heels. We often found her tearing up and down the hall, skidding a little and then pirouetting, just the way little lambs do. Weekends were a problem, and any little girl wanting to take Susie home had to produce a written invitation from her mother.

Helen holding Susie 1945

Some years later, Carleen had to have an operation, and as is the custom, the anaesthesiologist meets the patient the day before. The anaesthesiologist turned out to be Virginia Apgar, who originated the Apgar Score used on babies at birth the world over. Carleen and Virginia found that they were both listed as violists in the New Jersey pages of the Amateur Chamber Music Players' Directory. This was an immediate bond and they became very good friends.

Carleen is now internationally famous, having made well over 100 violas, plus violins, cellos and a few double basses. She has also made several sets of 8 stringed instruments, each one of a different size, starting with one smaller than a violin, including a vertical viola (to be played by a cellist) and going down to an oversized bass. Leopold Stokowksi took a great interest in her vertical violas, which have a wonderful, deep, rich resonance.

To my great surprise, all the labels inside of Carleen's instruments bear the word: SUS, the Latin for pig. I personally do not see the connection, but Carleen insists that there is a close connection between Susie Snowwhite and the beautiful instruments that she has made since then.

Helen Rice,

Excerpt from *DEVOTEE,* a "Magazine for Chamber Music Players and Listeners" Fall 1979 issue.

If historians record Elizabeth Sprague Coolidge as the "Fairy Godmother of Chamber Music," then somewhere it surely must be noted that Helen Rice has been its Ministering Angel. From the time of the founding of the Amateur Chamber Music Players, Helen Rice was its arch recruiter, record keeper, communicator, motivator, and indispensable pillar. All through the years, her relationship with the ACMP was 'a perfect marriage of the right person to the right calling'.

Paul Elisha, Editor
Troy, New York

As I think of Helen's world I realize more and more how greatly she will be missed, really the world over. I have never known anyone who made so many friends and who was so beloved by all. Ours was a truly wonderful friendship going back over forty years. How much we learned from her and how she widened our horizon, musically and otherwise.

Joe and I had such admiration and love for Helen and her mother that we named our daughter for them: Helen Margaret.

Lise Stein
Belmont, Massachusetts

I've known Helen all my life (I was named after her and her mother) and since most of our time together occurred as I was growing up, most of my memories are childhood ones. There was always a special aura about her and her house in Stockbridge, probably stemming from the deep affection between her and my father. I remember their long conversations on the porch, the trips to feed some very greedy fish under a bridge, a picnic high up on a windy hill, visits to botanical gardens, and of course, the music. When we girls were allowed to join the grownups in chamber music, she said, "It's a treat for you young people to play with us, but some day it will be a treat for us to play with you." As an adult, I did play with Helen and it was a treat for me too.

Helen Margaret Stein Skemer
Nutley, New Jersey

Helen with Joe Stein

In spite of Helen's sensitivity to pitch and dynamics, she managed easily to overlook a wobbly or slightly "off" note, a loss of place, or an all too vigorous bow as the price gladly paid in order to encourage active participation, especially when the sinner, whether young or old enough to know better, could be counted on to work for improvement. For many an individual, and the number must be very large, playing music with Helen, sharing in the actual production of beautiful sounds, marked the beginning of real enjoyment of music, the opening of doors to a whole art world.

Rustin McIntosh, M.D.
Tyringham, Massachusetts

Millicent McIntosh at a Brearley School celebration in her honor

Helen's sympathy with children was one of her most endearing qualities, even greater than her love of cats, which made her

138

the victim of many a lost, forlorn kitten. She loved to have children come to her home, and could always find and meet their greatest interest. The horse-crazy child would be taken to a nearby farm to see a new colt, and the restless boy would be popped into a friend's swimming pool. Those who could play instruments were encouraged to play, and others took part in her famous sessions with English hand bells. Even the youngest could sound his note with her help, and came away with a new sense of achievement.

Millicent McIntosh
Tyringham, Massachusetts

There is one aspect that is possibly not as well known to her music friends, and that is the close relationship that she had — emotionally — with the plant world. Of course everyone knew she had a vegetable garden. But did everyone know how much she loved it? I remember her saying to me, "I don't think people realize that I love gardening passionately." She gave away most of her produce — it was the growing that was important. I was pleased that she liked the variety of raspberries that grew in my garden, and she was delighted to have some of the canes. The pleasure she derived from those berries never waned — each year they were as much of a delight to her.

One spring she learned that we did not know about the spectacular mountain laurel on Mount Washington. She insisted on taking us there one morning. I will never forget the way she clambered over the rocks and pointed out the flowers to us. She went to see them each year, knew exactly where they were to be found, and took as much delight in them each time she saw them. But an equal part of the pleasure was to be able to share their beauty with others.

Do you remember the way she saved crusts of bread? When friends with young children came to visit she took them to the reservoir and let them feed the crusts to the fish, which surfaced to catch them. As much as the children enjoyed this, I think Helen enjoyed it equally.

Her understanding of children was also special. I remember that she was disappointed when friends with children called that they were coming to visit on a particular weekend. I was in her house when she received the call. She was disappointed, she told me afterwards, because on that particular weekend she was to

At the Reservoir 1973

have several guests, and would be too busy to spend much time with the children. She wanted them to come — but she wished to devote more time to them.

Everyone knew she loved cats. But this is a bit of information that is perhaps not known to others. On one of our trips to New York, she asked me to stop the car at a certain spot on the road. She disappeared for about ten minutes, and reappeared bringing me some wild catnip for my cats. Imagine knowing where that was to be found.

And the night-blooming cereus: I am so proud to have been given these wonderful plants. The way it came about was also typical of Helen. When we moved here, Helen asked if I could do her a favor and keep the plants in our greenhouse over the winter. Of course I was glad to do so. When she returned in the spring I offered to give them back to her. She came to see them, and said they were happier with me. Would I be good enough to keep them? Would I! She spoke as if I were doing her a favor, when of course I was the recipient of a wonderful gift. But we agreed that she would have visitation rights — she wanted to be called whenever there was a blossom. And since that was only at night, she would come when it was quite late to see the flower. Last summer when we had a record number of blooms — as many as nine in one evening — it was brought home to me most vividly that I am grateful to Helen for this too.

How do we explain to people who did not know her what her true legacy was? We all know it and feel it, but I for one am not clever enough with words to express it.

Louise Purvin
Stockbridge, Massachusetts

Just sitting down and thinking about Helen gives me such pleasure. Trying to catch even one thought and fasten it to paper isn't easy. I see her striking face; her sparkling, snapping eyes; her mouth and hear her saying all the encouragements to keep us playing, to have another sandwich, to keep one's eye on the ball and swing through. And isn't that just Helen! What a woman of purpose — a purpose cheerful, gracious, loving and constantly giving.

I leafed through my Greenwood journal and from forty years ago these are passages I wrote;

"Helen and Ruth took five of us over to Stockbridge. The garden is hardly bigger than Bunny's, but is packed full with everything. . . . We had a wonderful time."

"This afternoon instead of beaning I had a tennis lesson with Helen. It was wonderful. You always play so well with Helen."

". . . then Bunny let us have the remainder of the 'razberry' ice cream! Helen's 'razberries' are the best in the world!"

"This morning in the bean field Helen, Ruth and Paul came over. It was wonderful seeing them. We said good-bye to Helen. It was terrible seeing her leave. She's so wonderful."

Barbara Kunhardt
Amherst, Massachusetts

I want to say a few words about that most kind, civilized, gentle and purposeful woman who was a friend to so many of us, Helen Rice. I knew her from my first year at Greenwood, when I was 12 years old (1947) and went through reunions and many musical evenings in her wonderful home. I served as a fellow-Trustee and drove with her to Greenwood in the last few years as my children participated in the joyous Saturday night concerts, and Helen's enthusiasm waxed eloquent. She loved music and Greenwood and people.

141

I remember as a 12-year-old playing tennis with Helen. (Who is this elegant and proper lady who thinks she can play tennis with me?) Well, she beat the pants off me, all the while complimenting my every shot and each feeble attempt to return her meticulously placed strokes. Helen was a person who made this world a better place and showed us all by her example the best side of humanity.

Gilbert Kalish
New York City

In 1966 we were negotiating to buy a 15-room house, five bathrooms, closets, entrances, dressing rooms which in themselves could have served as spacious city apartments. The place was surrounded by 20 stately elms, all dead or dying, only we never noticed. We were city mice.

As we were concluding this somewhat impractical sale, we were told that there was a vegetable grower on the property, who in return for the use of our land would deliver all the fresh vegetables we wanted or needed, for free.

Not only were we proprietors of this huge house but we also had a tenant farmer on the property. It seemed like a good deal.

Our tenant farmer turned out to be an energetic white-haired smiler, Helen Rice to be exact, and our wonderful good fortune

In her Stockbridge garden

was to have a gardener on hand and who raised not only tomatoes, beans, squash (four kinds), spinach, lettuce (three kinds), peppers, Brussels sprouts, turnips, carrots and potatoes but also expanded the garden to include raspberries, gooseberries and currants. Year after year we were the happy recipients of her labors.

Helen's pleasure at making things grow was great. She was lucky. The garden work in the morning and evening was her tranquilizer in a very busy life filled with visitors and music. It was a rich, full life and I can remember her sometimes being angry but I never remember her being lonely.

Her physical strength (or perhaps it was simply will) seemed great. Although older than I, whenever a task involved a shovel or axe that I was wielding, she snatched the tool from me and proceeded herself to dig or chop with great energy. Here she was, an old lady really, digging, chopping in all weathers, and bringing the first beautiful pure red tomato to me every year.

She was so cheerful, hardworking and undemanding that I simply assumed she would go on working always. She never seemed to age. And in the process through the years and change of the seasons, I began to admire her and then to love her.

Helen spoke sometimes about her family and youth to me. There were different kinds of feuds in town. Helen once told me about her father's fury with the tennis club when they refused admission to a guest of his because he was Jewish. Helen said her father had a bitter battle with them. Of course this was at a time when such fights were practically unheard of and considered vulgar.

Then there was that famous bicycle feud, a difference of opinion as to whether bicycles should ride on the sidewalk or road. Helen's grandfather, as I remember it, felt that bicycles for the safety of pedestrians, should travel on roads. His adversary was one of the Sedgwicks, an old landed family in town. There was much publicity (it seems now hilarious) in the town newspaper and there was even some national publicity. "Of course," said Helen, "the Sedgwicks won; they were more powerful in town." I believe she retained some vestigial traces of anger at her grandfather's antagonists which only became dispelled as she began to play string quartets with the charming and musical Wohls. "Alice Sedgwick Wohl," she said, "is the best of the lot."

Bessie Klein
Stockbridge, Massachusetts

It was 1960 that I moved from Buenos Aires to N.Y. and being recommended from there to ACMP I called Helen and was immediately invited for a quartet session.

I never will forget my impression of warmth and being at home in Helen's presence, an impression which was growing every time when I met her.

But all the "Brandenburgs" and chamber music sessions were nothing in comparison with our time in Stockbridge where we had to be at least 2 days every time when we went to our summer stay in Maine. The trio- up to sextet-sessions were only topped by the kindness and warmth of this perfect hostess with her many interests; I was proud when I was allowed to connect the electric fence around her vegetable garden — against the raccoons — when she and my wife harvested string beans for our meal, when Millet's famous picture of the harvesting women came to my mind; I sent it to you and also a snapshot of the wonderful view from the porch with all the plants which grew so well at Helen's touch!

I miss her and I never will forget her!

William Winternitz
Jamaica Estates, New York

At Isle La Motte, Vermont

I wish that she were once more holding court as the Queen of chamber music and providing that unforgettable experience of making music together. I think back and remember her at Greenwood (I actually played with her); I remember her in Stockbridge and on the beach at Isle La Motte, the first Greenwood. But always I remember her with violin to her chin, telling me "If I can make it through this, you can!" I am privileged to have known her and to have touched the edge of her special world.

William A. Hill 3rd
Richmond, Vermont

70th birthday with Jay Rosenfeld and Stradivarius cake

Of course I remember Helen for her music — and for her tennis — but what I remember most fondly is the great care and attention she gave to her friends. She had the quality of being able to focus her whole self on the person she was with, communicating a friendship and kindness rare to behold. She conveyed the impression of perfect, accepting, selfless delight in other people. Always she seemed fresh in her caring. She was that way with everyone in my family, and she made them her family. It was her gift.

Steve Rosenfeld
Alexandria, Virginia

I first became acquainted with our friend Helen through an aunt of mine who had helped her out for two summers. My aunt became ill and asked me if I would be interested to meet Helen and perhaps help her out. The day I met Helen I knew I would enjoy helping her. That was back in 1962.

As the summers passed we became close friends. We had many enjoyable lunches together and Helen got so she talked to me about her parents and her life. She was always interested to hear about my family too, and she always made sure I met all her guests.

I always enjoyed seeing Helen go to her garden because she got so much pleasure out of the work and also in giving away her vegetables.

One day at lunch as we were talking, Helen said, "I think I can say one thing very few people can say. I have always been free to do as I wanted and when my time comes, I will have lived a really happy and fulfilled life." I will always remember her saying that.

Gertrude Seward
Sheffield, Massachusetts

At that time I was working as a photographer and it was obvious that this elegant person to whom I had been presented was as likely a subject as anyone I had ever met. After the sitting, as we walked back to our house, my father said 'that is as close to nobility as we come in this country.'

Steve Moore
Stockbridge, Mass.

I really can't remember a more evocative picture than the one in the Newsletter. Helen with all her energy intact but in a brief moment of rest. . There is something almost majestic about this picture, not because Helen ever bore herself that way but because there is more than a suggestion of just how splendidly a human being can turn out. And if all their majesties could be of this caliber, the world would be a better place.

Dick and Martha Snow
Bronxville, New York

Our daughter, Carolyn, who plays cello left-handed, played with Carl and Betty Williams at Miss Rice's one Christmas. Each wrote a greeting on a postcard sent to us.

We enjoyed so much Miss Rice's visit to Interlochen. One of her endearing traits was that she preferred playing 2nd violin.

Glen Halik
East Lansing, Michigan

The Rosenfeld family in Pittsfield

When I think of her, of her marvelous encouragement of whatever cello and tennis talents I had, of her coaxing and complimenting that drew always more out of me, of the grace of her ways, of the fabulous grace of her tennis strokes, of her personal way of getting her chin just right on the violin before playing, of her very distinct way of reacting to my father's jokes ("Oh, Jaaayyy"), of her forever white hair, of her rather small violin tone but always being "there," of her amazing patience with people, of so many things.

The one anecdote I always remember is when Mrs. Coolidge kept playing with her hearing aid while a quartet was reading Bartok in our house and how they had to reassure her that it wasn't the hearing aid but the music that was disturbing her.

Peter Rosenfeld
Leonia, New Jersey

My own memories of Helen obviously go back to my earliest childhood days. She spent a lot of time with us in New York. We visited in Stockbridge, and of course she was in Blue Hill a great deal, driving one of a series of touring cars and swimming twice daily! I am especially grateful to her for starting me as a squash player. When I was still in school in New York, she would invite me to meet her at the Cosmopolitan Club (strange place for a high school male!) and we would play this "new" game, which I continued in college, and later coached. When she was a "warden" at Bryn Mawr, I used to coax her out to play tennis once in a while, and I still vividly remember how strange I felt when I would occasionally escort a young Bryn Mawr damsel back to Rhoads Hall and be greeted by Helen in her official capacity!

I know that I was a great disappointment to her in one respect — she was always, in early years, trying to persuade me to start playing the cello, and I never quite succumbed. I will admit, as an aging adult, the fact that I never did learn to play an instrument is probably one of the real regrets of my life. I guess my parents never quite wanted to push me, especially after my brother Dicky died, because he did play the violin, so now I am a listener. All the above is obviously parenthetical.

Other memories include those of my mother and Helen playing four-hands, perhaps Brahms waltzes, with great gusto and much conversation. And *endless* conversations about music.

Helen's outstanding characteristic was *life*. What a vibrant personality she had — even in her Christmas cards there was such a wealth of enthusiasm and interest in *people*.

She certainly was a positive influence on our family for many years.

Charles Dethier
Wayne, Pennsylvania

My first meeting with Helen came about through tennis. In the summer of 1934, as each summer in those years, I entered several of the local club tennis tournaments held around New England. These were sociable affairs, with club families often providing rooms for out-of-town players. Helen was on the hospitality committee for the tournament held at the Wyantenuck Country Club, in Great Barrington, Massachusetts, near Stockbridge, and was present when the chairman read a letter from someone entering the tournament who requested that, if possible, he be housed

Pablo Casals and Edouard Dethier
Credit Margaret Rice

where it would not inconvenience his hosts if he practiced his viola between matches. Helen realized that the letter must be from the person whose dual interest in quartets and tennis she had heard about from Bunny Fay (Little), with whom (and with Ruth Mc-Gregor) I had played chamber music since 1929 (I was at Amherst College when they were at Smith). She invited me to play quartets during the tournament, and that began our forty-five-year friendship. I remember playing piano quartets that summer with Helen and the pianist Gunnar Johanson, then just coming onto the musical scene.

Helen was keenly interested in tennis herself, of course, and had a large collection of trophies from tournament play in tennis and squash racquets. Later that summer, she and I entered a mixed doubles tournament in Pittsfield, where we reached the

149

finals. She was used to mixing tennis and music, and used to play occasionally with the violinist Albert Spalding, who had an estate in Great Barrington. She also spoke of having played with Pablo Casals. During a trip to New York City one winter, in that period, I was invited to play squash racquets with Helen at the Cosmopolitan Club. I was a little diffident about playing squash with a woman, but she really played quite well. Helen wasn't diffident about it at all!

Samuel P. Hayes
Washington, D.C.

Sam and A.M. Hayes

My memory of Helen goes back to the spring of 1937, soon after my marriage to Sam. We were living in South Hadley, Massachusetts, where Sam was teaching at Mt. Holyoke, and we drove to Stockbridge several times for memorable quartet sessions. In the late spring, we learned that Helen was turning her 1929 Buick touring car in on a new car. The dealer offered her $50 on the trade-in, which she realized was ridiculous. When she told us about it, we jumped at the chance to get the car, which we needed and which was in fine condition, instead of letting the dealer get it for a song. We drove it to Chicago, where we were to spend the following year but, alas, Sam didn't get it winterized before a heavy freeze suddenly hit the city at Thanksgiving time and cracked the engine block. We sorrowed at the loss of a fine car and, equally, at the loss of Helen's tangible presence.

In the early spring of 1939, we were living in Bronxville, New York, in a studio apartment with a large, high living-bedroom. Sam had been acquiring second-hand chamber music for many years, and had an early edition of six Concerti Grossi by Corelli, a couple of Handel Concerti Grossi, and just one of the Brandenburgs (more later!), so I hit on the idea of organizing a concerto grosso evening. Walter Hendl, who, like Sam, was teaching at Sarah Lawrence College, conducted for us (thus launching what was to become an outstanding career as a conductor), and Helen was one of the players. She used to say in later years that it was this evening that gave her the idea for the Brandenburg evenings she held over the next forty years.

What I especially remember about Helen was her warmth and great kindness to everyone she met. She was particularly interested in young people, and the feeling was reciprocated. Both our children, Susan and Jonathan, were much attracted to Helen and always felt very close to her. Part of her attractiveness was, I think, because she was able to convey her genuine respect to each individual, no matter how young and inexperienced.

And then there was Helen's enthusiasm for her garden. She worked many long hours nurturing her large crops of vegetables, and then spent more hours delivering generous amounts to her friends. We were often beneficiaries of this largesse. We also enjoyed the late night calls that came to us at our home in Great Barrington when Helen's "Queen of the Night" cactus opened its blooms and spread its heavy fragrance on the air of her porch in Stockbridge.

Never a dull moment for Helen's friends!

A.M. Hayes
Washington, D.C.

As I sit down to write these reminiscences about Helen, the thought that she has forever vanished from my life is as acute and painful as at the time of her passing.

Helen had become a structural part of my intellect. Even when not visiting and playing chamber music with her, my wife and I would constantly think and talk about her. We had never encountered a person of such genuine human warmth and generosity.

We came to the United States as immigrants from Romania in the summer of 1965. Although a physician by training, music was an essential part of my life. In my family there were generations of professional and amateur musicians and I had a long experience of chamber music. Suddenly, after landing on these shores an oppressive vacuum set in for me, as I had no acquaintances at all in the world of chamber music players. Days in and days out I would briefly play my violin, but gone were the days when I would join my friends for quartets or string orchestra playing.

One day, one of our non-musician friends showed me an article in *Time* magazine which was telling the story of the Amateur Chamber Music Players and its secretary, Helen Rice.

I was thrilled. This was the miracle I was waiting for. How could I approach the "ebullient" secretary who had done so much for so many music lovers throughout the world? I decided to consult the telephone directory and, after trying several "Helen Rice"'s, I succeeded in introducing myself to Helen on the telephone and outlining with some timidity my musical credentials. Very shortly thereafter Helen invited me with my wife to her Manhattan apartment for a full evening of quartets. I know I played with a great deal of nervousness and insecurity. But Helen probably perceived my eagerness to play, and the rather unusual way of my discovering the Amateur Chamber Music Players made a lasting impression on her.

That evening, as I told her many times, was the evening that changed my life. For many years since, I was fortunate to play with Helen and her many friends numerous times up until two months before her death.

Helen was a unique human being whose greatest spiritual satisfaction was to help bring together people who shared intellectual affinities as well as their musical drive. As she said, in one of her letters which I treasure, "I keep saying over and over again how much I owe to the Amateur Chamber association. It has broadened my life immeasurably, and . . . it goes beyond the music."

As a physician, I was awed by the serenity with which Helen faced her death. She knew exactly the gravity of her disease and that her time was running out fast. Yet, she maintained to the very end her interest in people and in music. From her hospital bed she wrote me a letter in which she described to me her illness, but at the same time wanted to recommend that I meet and play with a talented violinist she had recently met.

I only wish that Helen knew how deeply her memory will be cherished by many thousands and that I will forever miss her.

Serban Fotino, M.D.
Ossining, New York

In doorway of Stockbridge house

Helen and I loved the Beethoven Opus 130, especially the Cavatina, and we made others play it as often as we could. Once I wrote about it and here it is.

Quatuor, #130, Cavatina.

"It contains all the tenderness and depth of feeling in human aspirations, and there is an anticipation, a reaching out for the relief of human tensions, and *getting* it. And it ends in a cry of exquisite pain and beauty."

Harold S. Belcher, M.D.
New York City

153

Greenwood Faculty Quartet
Helen Rice, Bunny Little, Margaret Clark, Ruth McGregor

During the summers of '40–'46 war years, when no one had enough gas to go anywhere, we at Greenwood in Cummington were lucky enough to have a permanent faculty string quartet. Lucky too, to have Helen Rice to lead it, to urge us on, to inspire us in pieces we knew, to introduce us to new works and to encourage us when we weakened.

Promptly at 4:30 every day we came in from the garden, the berry patch, the woods or wherever we had been working, set up chairs and stands in the big downstairs bedroom, to rehearse strenuously till supper. One or two evenings a week we moved out to the living room. There, just before bedtime, we played for the children sprawled on the floor — Haydn, Mozart, Beethoven. One summer we did all the Op. 18 quartets, one a week. Op. 95, the Schubert A minor and the great C major quintet with George Brown, our conductor (also a cellist) were all within our grasp when Helen was at the helm.

We all learned more from our work together than in any class in a college or conservatory. The excitement and fun we had has lasted through a lifetime of chamber music.

Bunny Little
Haydenville, Massachusetts

Helen took after her mother in disliking innovations. Mrs. Rice objected strenuously when Helen replaced the old coal stove with an electric one. Mrs. Rice had stoked the coal stove and carried out the ashes for years and didn't see why they needed a change. Then Helen herself resisted getting an electric dishwasher for Stockbridge even with the hordes of guests she fed all summer.

Mrs. Rice was a gracious and charming hostess, but after many years of listening to quartets in her living room she was not hesitant to voice an opinion. One evening after we finished reading a contemporary work from manuscript, Mrs. Rice said after a pause, "Is the composer a friend of anyone present?"

Helen often said that she had "marvellous parents" and Mrs. Rice once told me that Helen had inherited "all the best qualities from both sides of the family," that she was always "kind and gentle" although stubborn when she wanted her own way. Helen once told me that she was so docile as a child that when she was three her parents checked her "with the umbrellas" when they went to an Exhibition in Paris.

Mrs. Rice despaired of Helen's lack of interest in clothes. She once said to me "If Helen didn't have lovely hair and a beautiful complexion, my God how she'd look!" In a 1939 newspaper column after she had won a tennis tournament, the headline said "HATS A NUISANCE TO HELEN RICE" and continued "Merion tennis player wears same one the year 'round." Although Helen's only voluntary shopping was to buy blue jeans for the garden, she was appreciative of her friends' concern. She did say that she never noticed what anyone had on and didn't expect anyone to care what she wore.

Helen was fond of quoting Thomas Whitney Surette who, when asked whether he thought other people enjoyed their various pursuits as much as chamber music players did, answered that he thought not, because music was so many-sided. He summed it up by saying: "Music is physical, it is sociable, it is emotional, it is intellectual, and it is spiritual."

All through my quartet playing years with Helen, I marvelled at the way she put at ease even the most elementary or incompetent player. She would say "Oh, I did that badly" or "Could we do that again for my sake," thereby soothing the nervousness or boosting the confidence of the inexperienced player. It was a gift I have never seen duplicated.

Helen loved a good story. I remember arriving at her garden in Stockbridge, she with her hoe and I still in my "city clothes" while I described a trio session I had had the day before with a player piano. We had played the Mendelssohn d minor that begins with a cello solo. As I described trying to match my up-beat with the holes in the roll of the player piano, she laughed until the tears ran down her cheeks, and made me repeat the story many times.

Helen also saw the amusing side of some of her quartet-playing episodes. This is a quote from one of her letters:

"We had string quartets every evening and various other music during the day. They don't play brilliantly, but they *love* it and they are *so* nice! I wanted to show my appreciation so I presented them with a little music including the Ravel Quartet. Unfortunately they wanted to try it right away. You can imagine to a certain extent how it sounded with three not very strong players who knew it *not at all!* There were a few people on the sidelines and I rather suspect they suffered acutely. At moments it was *so* bad, intonation and one thing and another, that I could hardly keep from bursting out into wild gales of laughter. However, I managed to control myself and to remain unperturbed — outwardly!''

During all the years of her involvement with the ACMP the one thing that Helen was absolutely determined about was that there should be no fixed dues. Some board members tried to persuade her otherwise, but with no success. Her argument: "I'm one hundred per cent opposed to dues. Someone who can give only one dollar may need that evening of music more than anything else.''

It has been mentioned that Edwin T. Rice was awarded the Elizabeth Sprague Coolidge medal for his services to Chamber Music. Following in his footsteps, Helen was awarded, in 1980, Chamber Music America's first National Service Award, with the citation "To Miss Helen Rice who fostered our country's growing affection for chamber music through her dedicated leadership of the Amateur Chamber Music Players.''

In 1961 a new greenhouse was dedicated at the Berkshire Garden Center to Margaret Rood Rice, Helen's mother. Twenty years later a sturdy outdoor bench was placed in Helen's memory on the spot where she presided over the candy table at Harvest Festivals.

Helen was always amused at the way we met. Mr. Rice was a board member of the Society for the Publication of American Music and the auditions were held at the Rices' studio on West 67th Street. The judges gathered and listened to the new works performed by Juilliard students and others. I was studying cello at the Juilliard and Hans Letz was our quartet coach. On this

*Helen at dedication of greenhouse to Margaret Rood Rice, Berkshire Garden Center
1961*

occasion our quartet learned one of the new works, the composer's name a secret from us. Our quartet comprised three lively teenage boys and myself, already a Smith graduate. As the evening at the Rices' approached, Mr. Letz admonished us that we were going to a "very nice house and we should be sure to behave ourselves." Two things stand out about that evening (our piece didn't win). One was that Rubin Goldmark sat in the high-backed chair near the fireplace and during the program one of the Rices' cats leaped up from behind and landed on his bald head. The other indelible impression was that of our hostesses: Mrs. Rice with her beautiful white hair and regal bearing and her equally lovely golden-haired daughter Helen.

Ruth McGregor
New York City

Helen in 1941

ACMP DINNER HONORING HELEN RICE IN 1965

On October 29, 1965 a surprise dinner for Helen Rice was given in New York by the Amateur Chamber Music Players. More than 300 members attended, several of them from overseas. Since many readers of this book will not have seen the description of the dinner in ACMP's 1966 Newsletter, we reproduce here the talk by the principal speaker, Catherine Drinker Bowen and the drawing by Susan McIntosh Lloyd for the program cover.

CATHERINE DRINKER BOWEN

Ladies and Gentlemen. Friends of chamber music, friends of Helen Rice!

What an occasion this is, and what a party! How could anything be pleasanter than all of us meeting to honor Helen? Last spring, when this dinner was planned as a surprise party, I was deputed to write to Helen from Pennsylvania, where I live, and to inquire casually if she could play quartets at her house next October 29th in the evening. This seemed to me the wildest venture. Surely Helen knew that I am not one with a calendar requiring the making of such engagements four months in advance. But I wrote, any way. Helen replied with entire, and engaging innocence. But of *course* she'd save that evening, she said, and how delightful to make sure of it with four months to spare between!

Let me say that I have known Helen for nearly 30 years. And for nearly thirty years we have played chamber music together in all kinds of combinations, good combinations and — not so good combinations. (Helen is very charitable.) Tonight I am the final speaker in this symposium. And by now our guest of honor is tired of hearing her name, besides which she is by nature the last person to sit easily and listen to eulogy. So for my ten minutes — I was asked to speak for twenty and I shall speak for ten — for these minutes I am going to talk about Helen, and also about chamber music within and without our society.

When I was young and foolish I did not like that word, *amateur.* I thought of it as synonymous with not trying hard enough, synonymous with not being willing to take the personal risks your professional takes, or to make real sacrifices in order to attain real competence.

But I was wrong. A half century spent with music has proven it. There are persons whose lives touch and influence many other lives. Helen Rice, without ever turning to professionalism, wholly in an amateur capacity has enriched the lives of many, many people. Incidentally, one of the things I am fondest of in her ACMP Directory is the listing of grades:

A: Excellent
B: Good
C: Fair
D: Etc.

Now, just what does Etcetera mean? Isn't it wonderful? Surely its value lies in its vagueness, like the value of certain phrases in the United States Constitution, which were purposely left vague by the Founding Fathers — elastic words, capable of conforming to future circumstance.

When I first knew Helen, she was living on the Bryn Mawr College campus, in some kind of unnatural capacity as Warden of Rhoads Hall or something equally unsuitable. What she really was doing was teaching Bryn Mawr College to play chamber music. In those days, music simply had not taken hold at Bryn Mawr. Helen's was a voice crying in the wilderness. But she succeeded. She organized chamber music and got those girls to playing. If anyone could do it, Helen could. I lived close by and observed the proceedings for three years, including the afternoon when we were to play piano quartets for a summer school session and found the best piano locked. The best piano was for solos, it devolved. The second best, tuned or untuned, would do for ensemble.

I wish I had kept track of the places where Helen and I have played together. We have played in Connecticut and in New York, in Bryn Mawr, Haverford and Merion — along what is known as the Main Line of the Pennsylvania Railroad. We have played in Stockbridge, Massachusetts and in Tyringham. The list could go on and on. When Helen telephones me to come somewhere and play, I can no more resist than I can resist breathing. Always, afterward, I come away from these sessions feeling I have learned something. Learned to use less bow in the rapid passages, learned how to play those measures in the Mozart D minor, where the second violin repeats the sextolet figure.

From time to time I have had the privilege of playing with Helen and Ruth McGregor and Mariana Lowell Barzun, all members of our Association. The night before, I can't sleep because I am nervous, they're such good players. The night after, I don't sleep because I am so happy.

And may I say also that I have played quartets with Helen at times that were fateful and unhappy for me. My mother died at the age of 86, after a life fulfilled. The evening of the day she died, Helen's quartet, of which I was a member, happened to be playing just around the corner. I telephoned to ask if I might come and play as usual, I said I could not think of anything more comforting — or more congenial to my mother's memory, for she had loved chamber music.

You will forgive me for mentioning anything so personal, and for speaking of sad times in so gay a company. But the playing of chamber music is for many of us, so deep an experience, a spiritual release so effectual that perhaps it is well to speak of it in serious and emotional terms.

I wonder how many of you who have reached the age of say, fifty, are asked the question I have been asked now for many years. Strangers ask it, and old friends not seen in a long time. "Do you," they say, "still play the violin?"

Perhaps this is a way of inquiring politely if one finds oneself well, or if one has commenced as yet to disintegrate. In Seattle, Washington, about fifteen years ago, I was sitting in the front row of a college auditorium waiting to go on stage and lecture about history. A man came down the aisle and tapped me on the shoulder. He was in a hurry. He told me he had come from one of the islands in the lake, a long way off, and that he had read my little book, Friends and Fiddlers. "I can't stay for your lecture," he said. "I just came to ask one question: *Mrs. Bowen, do you still play?*"

I said of course I did. The man shook me heartily by the hand, said that's all he wanted to know, and disappeared up the aisle. I wonder if that man is a member of our society. I hope he is.

Out of mercy to our friend Helen, I am talking now about chamber music in general terms, but terms which I believe lie within the experience of most of you. . . . One thing I must mention, one by-product of chamber music playing which now enhances my suburban domicile. Not long ago one of our members, Carleen Hutchins, the viola maker, came to Haverford and hung the most enchanting object against the ceiling of my hallway: a *mobile,* made of the shells, the outside rims and shapes of violins, violas, and the fill-in parts of F holes. She said they were leftovers from her workshop. The mobile is suspended and balanced from the sticks of two violin bows. At the slightest breath of air it turns lightly, with grace and dignity. It is perfectly enchanting. I invite any of you, passing by, to come and see it. And I owe this, too, obliquely to Helen, for it was she who introduced me to Mrs. Hutchins.

Helen Rice! It makes me very proud to stand before all these players, and testify to what you have done for music and for all of us. To you, more than anyone, the A.C.M.P. owes its continued existence. I have been a guest in your house when chairs and tables overflowed with newsletters to be mailed, problems about addresses and about recalcitrant members who did not send in their names. I know the hours of hard labor you have put in on our behalf, from here to Yugoslavia.

Tonight we honor not only your hard work but your inspiration, the drive, the generosity of that quiet, attractive, invincible and staunch personality.

Drawing by Susan McIntosh Lloyd
for the program cover

REMARKS AT MEMORIAL SERVICES 1980

Helen's circle of friends included many professional players. It was very fitting that a number of these played at the two Memorial services for her in 1980: the Juilliard Quartet in New York on April 29 and a trio of friends, Sonya Monosoff, Burton Fine, and Peter Rosenfeld at the Tyringham service on June 29th near her Stockbridge home. Her long-time friends, Millicent McIntosh and Samuel P. Hayes spoke at both services and were joined by Roy Boutard of the Berkshire Garden Center, in Tyringham. We reprint excerpts from their remarks here.

Remarks of Samuel P. Hayes

Mrs. McIntosh and I plan to highlight today some of the diverse facets of Helen's life — and her outlook on life — as we came to know them. Mrs. McIntosh will focus on facets other than music, and I on the musical. Of course, we will overlap somewhat, because Helen's many interests and activities were so intertwined.

Before turning to Helen's music, let me touch on one aspect of her life that colored much of the rest. This was the solid roots she had planted — and never pulled up — in her native Manhattan and almost-native Stockbridge. Helen was one of those rare individuals who never changed her physical and psychological base. Except for her four years as a college student at Bryn Mawr and her later three years there as a "warden" and chamber music coach, she lived for 75 years in the apartment her parents owned in Manhattan. And, except for some summers at a music colony in Maine and many trips abroad, she spent all her summers in the home her grand-parents built last century in Stockbridge, where her parents were married.

Music was, of course, the keynote of Helen's life — at least after her college years. She learned early to play the violin but, by her own account, didn't get fired up about chamber music until after college, despite having been, as a youngster, impressed into service as second violinist with the very good musicians her cello-playing, lawyer father frequently brought to their apartment.

In her twenties and thirties, Helen developed her musical skills — as well as other skills — to a high level. She gave a great deal of time to playing music with a wide variety of people, and to teaching as well — at the Brearley School, where she was Chairman of the Music Department; at Bryn Mawr; and at the Greenwood Music Camp, where she taught both music and tennis for 7 years in the 1940's.

Playing music with Helen was highly rewarding. Her knowledge of the literature was extensive, and her musical taste impeccable. Because she knew so thoroughly what was going on — and what should be going on — in all the voices, each person playing with her felt challenged to do his or her best, and usually did. Her leadership was confident and kept the group together. Yet, she was meticulous in offering to alternate the first violin part with whatever other violinist was playing, even one far less adept in technique or experienced in leadership than she.

Helen, herself, was the ultimate in an amateur musician. With a high level of knowledge, skill and musicianship, she played for the love of it, and for the love of playing with others. This did not mean, however, that she cut herself off from professional music. Quite the contrary. She admired professionals greatly, frequented their performances, and encouraged and helped them as she could. She recognized professional music as the acme of the art, but she valued amateurs too, because, as players and not just listeners, they bring added appreciation and responsiveness to musical audiences. Thus, she saw amateurs and professionals as two sides of a single coin. One could not flourish without the other.

It was when Helen was in her forties that the Amateur Chamber Music Players was formed, at a meeting in her apartment, and she agreed to become its Secretary — on the model of the British "Honorary Secretary". The rest, needless to say, is history! The idea was intrinsically a good one — that amateurs away from home needed some way to find other amateurs eager to play music; and a directory of chamber music players, kept up to date, would meet this need. But the idea could go nowhere without intelligent and imaginative guidance and a lot of plain hard work. For 33 years, Helen, with Ruth McGregor as Treasurer for most of those years, provided the guidance, the energy and the hard work. Helen wrote personal notes to all new members, often hundreds a year. She prepared the annual newsletter. She took innumerable telephone calls, invited countless strangers to play music with her in New York or Stockbridge, and gave food and drink to literally thousands of players and listeners.

Helen's generous interest in all and sundry was legendary. She loved people. She wanted to know not only about one's musical interests but also about one's family, work, and views about the world. Helen's Stockbridge home was often full for weeks at a time, with old friends and new, playing music, eating Helen's meals (in which her home-grown vegetables played a major role), and sleeping in Helen's numerous beds. The beds were occasionally strained to match her hospitality, though. On at least one occasion, with all the beds committed to others, Helen tried to sleep on a settee on the porch. I say "tried", because one guest was so enthused that he practiced his 'cello in the living room, next to the porch, until 2:00 a.m., not noticing when Helen tip-toed by in her dressing gown!

So many people have enjoyed Helen's hospitality, played music in groups she organized, developed their skills in classes she coached, and drawn inspiration from her example, that Helen must surely have come to preside over one of the largest families in history! This family, and the thousands of other chamber musicians who related to it in various ways, now together constitute an enduring testament to Helen's imagination, inspiration and continued effort. This testament is the Amateur Chamber Music Players, now very much a going concern. No one could hope for a more impressive and durable memorial!

Fortunately, the ACMP did not hide its gratitude and esteem until too late. In 1965, several hundred members attended a surprise dinner in New York City, to pay tribute to Helen. At that time, in addition to remarks by Catherine Drinker Bowen and others, Helen was presented with a large collection of letters of warm appreciation.

Remarks of Millicent McIntosh

I first knew Helen in 1919 when she was a Freshman at Bryn Mawr and played fullback on the Varsity hockey team. She was a tower of steadiness and strength. That winter, we played opposite each other in class water polo matches, and I can still see the long, accurate throws she made into our goal, from the far corners of the pool. In the spring, she was Number One on the Varsity tennis team, a natural happening for one who won the Stockbridge Ladies' Singles at 14, and had a national rating for years.

We next came together in the summer of 1934, when Rusty and I rented a house in Tyringham, before we found our present home. She often bicycled from Stockbridge to play music nearby, and we became aware at that time of her skill and her matchless enthusiasm. As our family grew, she was very important to us all, coming to encourage our five fledgling musicians by playing with them, and doing the same thing for our twins on the tennis court.

Helen's garden was a delight to her, especially when she could share her produce with her friends. She brought and installed in our garden enough raspberry plants to provide us lavishly through the years. Each summer, she also raised and carried car-load after car-load of garden produce to the Greenwood Music Camp at Cummington.

Helen was a skillful carpenter, and made the tables and benches for Greenwood. Later, she brought us a fire bench which she had carved at both ends. During the war, when farmhands were in short supply, she went at dawn and late afternoon almost every day to help a neighboring farmer milk the cows.

Last August, our youngest son, Dick, now a biologist at the University of Colorado, asked Helen if it would be possible for his family of five to stay with her if they came to New York for their spring vacation. She was delighted to have them, and it was arranged that three could have beds and two sleep in sleeping bags in the studio. Although she was in the hospital having tests, she made it very clear that she didn't want to call them off. She arrived home the day before they came in. They were able to market for her and cook dinner, and she seemed to enjoy the children very much. She told me that Craig, who is ten, would come and talk with her at breakfast while the others were asleep. He said that he loved to put his sleeping bag under her piano; that the things he liked best about New York were the Natural History Museum and her apartment. The last night they were there, Ruth McGregor arranged to bring one of her pupils to play quartets. Craig, who has recently started the violin, played along with her, and afterwards said to Helen, "I think I have at last broken into the chamber of music."

Remarks of C. Roy Boutard, in Tyringham

I remember Miss Rice for her great love of gardens. Not only was Miss Rice an active board member of the Garden Center, she was also a great friend and ambassador, helping us out by volunteering for many different functions.

Whenever she had house guests, who seemed to come from all over the world, she never missed a chance to show them the Garden Center. She was keenly interested in Queen of the Night cactus plants and presented us with an offspring of the nocturnal Queen Mother which resided in her New York apartment. When we were later offered a good steel-framed greenhouse from Williamstown, Miss Rice helped with the cost of moving and reconstruction and we dedicated the house to her mother, Margaret Rood Rice. The Queen of the Night got a wall for support and one day when we were certain that it was going to bloom in abundance we announced the event in the paper and two hundred people came to watch the twenty-two strongly-scented flowers gradually open. To predict the exact opening of the flowers is very difficult, as they are very sensitive to temperature changes and maybe even atmospheric pressures. I once called up Miss Rice just before midnight, after she had gone to bed, but she came down like a shot to watch the "blooming". When I apologized for the late hour she said, "Mr. Boutard, I never mind being wakened for the Queen of the Night."

It will seem strange not to have Miss Rice at this year's Harvest Festival, selling her delicious home-made fudge. "Put me in the shade," she always said, "or the candy will melt." I never gave her enough shade for I could not bring myself to put a person with such a sunny disposition in the shade.

CHAMBER MUSIC PLAYED AT
HELEN RICE'S DOMICILES

Her New York Studio
Her home in Stockbridge
Her Bryn Mawr College residence (as Warden)

Helen Rice started to keep her music diaries in 1934. As her father had done before her, she listed under each date the names of the participants and the chamber music played. We list here the composers and their works played at Helen's (New York, Stockbridge, and Bryn Mawr) over the years. Since her famous Brandenburgs fall outside of the chamber music category, they are not included here. Wind players will note that the list is heavily weighted toward string chamber music except where compositions include both winds and strings: flute quartets, clarinet quintets, Beethoven septet, Schubert octet, etc. Contemporary music occupies a rather limited space for various good reasons.

The following list has been checked with Cobbett's Encyclopaedia of Chamber Music for accuracy of opus numbers, keys, etc. Music not found in Cobbett remains as Helen entered it in her diaries.

Absil, Jean
    Suite, vc, pf (20th C Belgian)
Albrechtsberger
    Duos, v, vc
    Quartet, str, A
d'Ambrosio
    Quartet, str, c mi, Op. 42
Antoine-Barthelemy, Bruno
    Duos, v, vla, Vol. 1
Arensky
    Quartet, v, vla, 2 vc, Op. 35
Arriaga
    Quartet, str, d mi, No. 1

Bach, C.P.E.
    Quartet, str, D, No. 1
    Quartet, str, D, No. 4
Bach, J.C.
    Trio, v, vla, vc, A
    Quintet, 2 cl, 2 horns, fag, No. 3

Bach, J.S.
  Sonatas (ALL) v, pf
  Sonatas, (ALL) gamba, pf
  Sonatas, 2 v
  Duos, v, vla
  Trio Sonatas, G, d mi
  Canon alla Decima, v, vla (from Art of Fugue)
  Quartet, Art of the Fugue, str
  Musical Offering — 6-part fugue
  Motet "Lobet Den Herrn"
  Motet "Jesu, Meine Freude"
Bach, W.F.
  Duos, 2 vla, No. 2 & 3
Barber, Samuel
  Sonata, vc, pf, Op. 6
Bargiel
  Quartet, str, d mi, Op. 47, No. 4
Bartok
  Sonata, v, pf, Op. 18
  18 Duos, 2 v (or 2 vc)
  Quartets, str, No. 1, 2, 4, 5
Beach, Mrs. H.H.A.
  Songs
Beethoven
  Sonatas (ALL) v, pf
  Sonatas (ALL) vc, pf
  Trios (ALL) pf, v, vc
  Trios (ALL) str
  Quartets (ALL) str
  Duos, v, vla (Music for Two — Music Press)
  Duo, vla, vc "Augenglasern"
  Trio, Serenade, fl, v, vla, Op. 25
  Duos, three, v, vc (orig. cl, fag)
  Quintet, 2 vla, C, Op. 29
  Quintet, 2 vla, Op. 104 (from c mi trio, Op. 1, No. 3)
  Quintet, 2 vla, Fugue, Op. 137
  Sextet, wind, 2 cl, 2 horns, 2 bassoons (also arranged for
      strings) Op. 71
  Septet, cl, horn, bassoon, v, vla, vc, bass, Op. 20
Bloch, Ernest
  Quartet, str, four "Night Pieces"
Boccherini
  Sonata, vc, pf, A

Sonata, 2 vc, C (Bazelaire)
Quartets, str, No. 1, 4, 8
Quintets, 2 vc, C (conglomerate), E, g mi
Boismortier
Sonata, 2 vc
Bonelli
Quartet, str, Op. 28, No. 2
Borodin
Quartets, str, A; No. 2, D; Nocturne
Brahms
Sonatas (ALL), v, vla, vc, cl, with pf
Trios (ALL), pf, v, vc; horn trio, Op. 40; cl trio Op. 114
Quartets (ALL), pf v, vla, vc
Quintet, pf, f mi, Op. 34 2 vl, vla, vc
Quintets, 2 vla, Op. 88; Op. 111
Quintet, cl, Op. 115
Sextet, 2 v, 2 vla, 2 vc, B flat, Op. 18
Sextet, 2 v, 2 vla, 2 vc, G, Op. 36
Songs
Brant, Henry
"True Strings" for Hutchins violin family
Bridge
Sonata, v, pf
Quartet, str, e mi (fun to play)
Quintet, pf, d mi
Sextet, str, 2 v, 2 vla, 2 vc
Bruckner
Quintet, 2 vla, F
Quintet, 2 vla, Intermezzo
Busoni
Sonata, v, pf, e mi, No. 2
Byrd
2 Fantasias, 2 fl, str
Fantasia, v, vla, 2 vc
Fantasies, 6 instr, c mi, e mi, No. 1, 2

Catoire
Sonata, v, pf, b mi, Op. 15
Trio, pf, f mi
Castelnuovo-Tedesco
Sonata, vla, vc
Chausson
Concerto for v, pf and str quartet, Op. 21

Cherubini
    Quartet, str, C, No. 2
Chopin
    Sonata, vc, pf, g mi, Op. 65
Cole
    Quartet, ob (British)
Coleman, R
    Variations on "Happy Birthday"
Corigliano, John
    Sonata, v, pf
Couperin
    Vc, str quartet "Pièces de Concert" (Bazelaire)
    Quintet, 2 v, 2 vc, pf "La Sultane"
Debussy
    Sonata, v, pf
    Sonata, vc, pf, d mi
    Quartet, str, Op. 10
De Large
    Trio, pf (Dutch)
De La Marter, Eric
    Trio, pf, "Apple Tree"; "Serenade"
Delius
    Sonatas, v, pf, No. 1, 3
    Quartet, str, No. 2
Dello Joio
    Trio, pf
Dittersdorf
    Trio, 2 v, vc
    Quartets, 6, str
    Quintet, 2 vc, No. 1
Dohnanyi
    Sonata, v, pf, Op. 21
    Trio, pf, Serenade
    Trio, str, v, vla, vc, Op. 10, Serenade
    Quartets, str, 3
    Quintet, pf, Op. 1, No. 1
    Quintet, pf, Op. 26
Donizetti
    Quartet, str, D, No. 4
Dont
    Trio, 2 v, vc
Durand, Robert
    Quartet, str, Haitian Themes

Dushkin, Dorothy
    Quintet, ob, str. "For Amanda"
Dvorak
    Sonata, v, pf, Op. 57
    Trio, pf, Dumky, Op. 90
    Terzetto, 2 v, vla, Op. 74
    Quartets (ALL), str
    Quintet, pf, Op. 81
    Quintet, 2 vla, Op. 97
    Sextet, str, A, Op. 48

Elgar
    Sonata, v, pf, Op. 82
    Quartet, str, Op. 83
Elsmith, Leonard
    Quartet, str, Folk Dance Tunes
Enesco
    Octet, str, Op. 7

Fauré, Gabriel
    Sonata, v, pf, No. 2
    Trio, pf, Op. 120
    Quartet, pf, c mi, Op. 15
    Quartet, pf, g mi, Op. 45
    Quartet, str, Op. 121
    Quintet, pf, Op. 89
    Quintet, pf, Op. 115
Fehr, Fred
    Quartet, str, "Birthday Joke"
Fotino
    Sonata, v, pf
Franceschini, G.
    Quartet, 2 v, vc, pf
Franck, César
    Sonata, v, pf (also vc) A
    Trio, pf, Op. 2
    Quartet, str, D
    Quintet, pf, f mi
Frescobaldi
    Quartet, pf (?), Canzoni No. 1, 2
Fuchs, Robert
    Trio, 2 v, vla, Op. 61 No. 2

172

Fux, J.J.
    Sonata, v, vla (?) Canon

Gassman
    Trio, 2 v, vla, B flat
Gastoldi
    Duo, v, vla — Music for Two (Music Press)
Gehot, Joseph
    Trios, str
Giardini
    Quartet, str, Op. 29 No. 1
Gibbons
    Quartet, str, Fantasia No. 1
    Quintet, str, Pavane & Gailliard
Glazounow
    Quartet, str, Op. 15 Novelettes
    Quintet, 2 vc, A, Op. 39
Glière
    Ten Pieces, 2 vc, Op. 53
    Quartet, str, A, Op. 2
    Sextet, str, Op. 7
Gluck
    Sonata à trois, 2 v, pf, g mi
Goldstein, David
    Pieces, recorder, 3 str
Grieg
    Sonata, vc, pf, a mi, Op. 36

Handel
    Sonatas (ALL), v, pf
    Sonatas (ALL), 2 v
    Sonatina, v, vla (Halvorsen)
    Suites, 2 v, vc
    Fugue, fl, v, vc, F
Haydn, F.J.
    Quartets (ALL), str
    Trios (ALL), pf
    Duos, 2 v
    Duos, v, vla "Music for Two" (Music Press)
    Duos, vla, vc
    Trio, str, Divertimenti
    Trios, 2 fl, vc, London Trios
    Trio, fl, v, vc
    Trio, Barytone (?)

Haydn, Michael
    Quintet, vla, G, Op. 88
de Hervelois, Caix
    Suite, vc, pf
Herzogenberg
    Quintet, 2 vla, c mi, Op. 77
Hindemith
    Sonata, v, pf Op. 11 No. 2
    Quartet, str, No. 1, Op. 10
    Quartet, str, No. 3, Op. 22
    Quartet, str, "Acht Stuecke" Op. 44
    Quintet, cl, 2 v, vla, vc, Op. 30 Variations
Honegger
    Sonata, v, pf, No. 1
    Quartet, str, soprano "Pâques à New York"
Hummel
    Sonata, vla, pf
    Duos, 2 vla
    Trio, str, E flat (posth)

Ibert
    Quartet, str
d'Indy
    Quartet, str
    Quartet, pf, Op. 7
Ives
    Sonata, v, pf
    Quartet, str, No. 1

Jacobi Frederick
    Fantasy, vla, pf
Jadin, Hyacinthe
    Quartet, str, No. 3 (excellent)
Kodaly
    Sonata, vc, pf, Op. 4
    Quartet, str, Op. 2, No. 1
Krommer
    Nonet

Lawes, William
    Sextet: Fantasy and Air
Lazzari
    Sonata, v, pf, e mi Op. 24

174

Leclair
Duos, 2 v
Duo, v, vla Music for Two (Music Press)
Locatelli
Quintet, pf "Symphony"
Locke, Matthew
Fantasia, 4 viols No. 6
Lockwood, Normand
Six Nocturnes (?)
Loeffler
"Music for Four Strings"
Loeillet
Sonatas, 2 v, D, G
Trio Sonata, Op. 1 No. 1
Trios, pf, G, b mi
Quartet, pf, b mi

Malir, Frantisek
Quartet, str, Pieces
Manuel, Roland
Trio, 2 vla, vc, or v, vla, vc
Martin, F
Trio, str
Martinu
Duos
Trio, str Madrigals No. 1
Trio, No. 3, 4 Bergerettes
Quintet, 2 vla
Sextet
Mason, Daniel Gregory
Sonata, v, pf, g mi Op. 5
McDowell, Jack
Trio, pf
Mendelssohn
Trios, pf, Op. 49, 66
Quartets (ALL), str
Quintet, str (2 vla) Op. 18
Quintet, str (2 vla) Op. 87
Sextet, pf, v, 2 vla, vc, bass Op. 110
Octet, str, Op. 20
Milhaud
Sonatina, v, vla

Trio, str
Suite, cl, v, pf
Moore, E
Duo, v, vc
Morley
Music for Two (Music Press) v, vla
Mozart, Leopold
Divertimenti, 2 v, vc
Mozart, W.A.
Sonatas (ALL), v, pf
Trios (ALL), pf
Duos (ALL), v, vla K487
Quartets (ALL), str
Quintets (ALL), vla
Divertimento, v, vla, vc, E flat, K563
Trio, cl, vla, pf K498
Divertimento, 2 v, vla (2 cl, fag) No. 3
Quartet, ob K370
Quartets, fl K285, 298
Quartets, pf, K478, 493
Quartets, str, 3 Divertimenti (Salzburg Symph)
Quintet, cl K581
Quintet, horn K407
Serenade, 8 winds, No. 12, K388
Mysliweczek, Joseph
Quartet, pf

Nielsen
Quartet, Op. 44 (?)
Novak
Quartet, str, G, Op. 22, No. 1
Quartet, str, D, Op. 35, No. 2
Onslow
Quartet, str, g mi, No. 7
Parker, Horatio
Suite, pf, v, vc, A, Op. 35
Payne, John Knowles
Quartet, str, Variation
Pischl
Duo, v, vla, F
Pergolese
Sonata, v, pf, E
Sonata, vc, pf
Septet, f mi

Phillipps, Burrill
    Duo Dialogue
    Pieces, fl, v, cl, vc
Pierné
    Sonata, v, pf, d mi Op. 36
    Quintet, pf, Op. 41
Piston, Walter
    Duo
Platti
    Duo, vla, vc
Porter, Quincy
    Quartet, str, No. 6
Prokofieff
    Sonata, v, pf, D No. 2
    Quintet, v, vla, ob, cl, bass Op. 39
    Sextet, cl, str quartet, pf, Op. 34 "Overture on Yiddish Themes"
Purcell
    Sonata, 2 v, No. 3
    Sonata, ,Golden, 2 v, pf
    Fantasias in Four Parts, No. 4, 5, 6, 7
    Quartet, str Chaconny
    Quartet, str Fantasia
    Suite, fl (ed. Malcolm Holmes) str
    Quintet, 2 v, 2 vla, vc — Fantasia on One Note

Rameau
    Duo, v, vla "Music for Two" (Music Press)
Rawsthorne
    Quartet, cl, str
Ravel
    Trio, pf, a mi
    Quartet, str, F
Reger
    Suite in alten style, v, pf Op. 93
    Sonata, vc, pf
    Trio, pf Op. 102
    Trio, str Op. 77B
    Serenade, fl, v, vla (or 2 v, vla) Op. 77A
    Serenade, fl, v, vla (or 2 v, vla) Op. 141A
    Quintet, cl, A Op. 146
    Quintet, pf Op. 64
    Sextet, str, F Op. 118

Reicha
   Quintet, ob, str
Reinhold, Hugo
   Quintet, 2 vc Op. 10
Respighi
   Quartet, str "Antiche Danze"
Rheinberger
   Quintet, pf, C Op. 114
Riegger, W
   Variations (Duo?)
Ries
   Quintet (one of three)
Rogers, Patsy
   "Family of Strings" for Carleen Hutchins' violins
Rolla
   Duos, 2 v
Rolland
   Trio, str
Rossini
   Quartet, str, E No. 5 (much merriment)

Sandby
   Quartet, str No. 2
Sanders
   Trio, 2 v, vla (dedicated to H.R.)
Scarlatti
   Sonatas, v, pf
Schäffer, H
   Nocturne, 8 vc
Schmitt, Florent
   Quintet, pf, b mi Op. 51
Schoenberg
   Sextet, str (Verklärte Nacht) b mi Op. 4
Schubert
   Sonatina, v, pf No. 1
   Duo, v, pf
   Trios, pf, v, vc B flat, Op. 99
   Trios, pf, v, vc E flat, Op. 100
   Quartets (ALL), str
   Quintet (Forellen), v, vla, vc, cb, piano, A Op. 114
   Quintet (Cello) C, Op. 163
   Octet, 2 v, vla, vc, cb, cl, fag, horn Op. 166

Schumann
 Sonata, v, pf, a mi No. 1
 Trio, pf, d mi Op. 63 No. 1
 Trio, pf, Four Phantasiestücke Op. 88
 Fairy Tales, cl, vla, pf Op. 132
 Quartets, str Op. 41, a mi, F, A
 Quartet, pf Op. 47
 Quintet, pf Op. 44
Sechter, Simon
 Duo, vla, vc
Shostakovich
 Quartet, str, C No. 1
 Quartet, str, D No. 6
 Quartet, str, c mi No. 8
Sibelius
 Quartet, str, "Voces Intimae" Op. 56
Sinding
 Quintet, pf Op. 5
Smetana
 Quartet, str, e mi Op. 116 No. 1
 Quartet, str "Aus Meinen Leben" No. 2
Sokoloff
 Quartet, str (one of three)
Spohr
 Duo, Grand, e mi, v, vla
 Octets, str, Op. 65 & 87 (Op. 65 excellent)
Stamitz
 Duo, Op. 19 No. 1
 Quartet, cl, str Op. 8 No. 4
Stein, Ernest
 Trio, str
Sterkel
 Duos, three, 2 vla
Stevens, Halsey
 Duos, five, 2 vc
Stoessel
 Suite, 2 v, pf, D "In Antique Style"
Strauss, R
 Sonata, v, pf, E flat, Op. 18
 Quartet, str, A Op. 2
Stravinsky
 Sonata, v, pf
Svendsen

Octet, str, A Op. 3
Szymanowski
    Quartet, str, C Op. 37

Taneiev
    Trio, str, 2 v, vla, D Op. 21
Tartini
    Sonata, v, pf, g mi
Taylor, Coleridge
    Quintet, cl, f sharp mi Op. 15
Tchaikowsky
    Trio, pf, a mi Op. 50
    Quartet, str, D Op. 11
Telemann
    Sonata, fl, harpsichord, f mi
    Suite, fl, vla
    Sonatas, vla (arr. Louise Rood)
    Trio Sonatas, D, F
    Quartet, str, Suite, G
    Tafelmusik, fl, ob, vc, cembalo
    Tafelmusik, v, fl, vc, cembalo
Toch
    Serenade, 2 v, vla Op. 25
Tompkins
    Suite, pf, 2 v, vla, vc
    Fantasias in six parts
Turina
    Quartet, str, d mi "Prayer of the Toreador"

Veracini
    Sonata, 2 v
    Sonata a tre, 2 v, vc, pf, c mi Op. 1
Vieuxtemps
    Quartet, str, e mi Op. 44
Villa Lobos
    Bachianas Brasileiras, 8 vc No. 1
Vivaldi
    Sonata, v, pf, g mi
    Sonata, 2 v, d mi
Volen, Fortein
    Quartet, str, Op. 13
Vycpálek, L
    Duo, v, vla

Walton
    Quartet, pf, v, vla, vc
Warlock, Peter
    Songs
Webern
    Quartet, str, Six Bagatelles Op. 9
    Quartet, str, Five Pieces Op. 5
Williams, Vaughan
    "On Wenlock Edge" voice, pf, str
    Quartet "To Jean"
    Quartet "100th Psalm"
    Quintet, 2 v, 2 vla, vc Fantasy
Wikmansen (sp?)
    Quartet No. 2
Wolf, Hugo
    Quartet, str, d mi "Italian Serenade"
    Songs

Zimbalist
    Sonata, v, pf, g mi (1924)

NAMES OF PEOPLE WHO PLAYED
CHAMBER MUSIC AT HELEN'S

Again, from Helen's music diaries, we list the names of those who played chamber music with her. We regret that space did not permit including the hundreds who played only at the Brandenburg evenings. If some names are incomplete, it is because they were listed that way.

Abel, Theodora
Abetti, Betty
Ackerman, Ruth
Adam, Claus
Adams, Jean
Agus, I.
Ajemian, Anahid
Alexander, Ben
Alexieff, Vladimir
Allison, Miss
Alperin, Nettie
Alwyn, Horace
Anastasio, Richard
Anderson, Helen
Andres, Emily
Annas, Helene
Annavedder, Ed
Ansbacher, Charles
Apgar, Lawrence
Apgar, Virginia
Applebaum, Sandra
Archibald, Miss
Arens, Michael
Armstrong, A.
Arnt, Mr.
Ash, Herman
Assmussen, Hans
Atkins, John
Aub, Elizabeth
Auerbach, Ernest
Auerbach, Lee
Auger, Amy
Austin, John
Aylesworth, R.

Bach, Erika
Bacon, Helen

Baer, Georgette
Bargarotti, Mr.
Bailey, Parker
Baker, Katharine Gratwick
Ballard, Mrs.
Ballou, Melinda Carol
Ballou, Persis
Ballou, Steven
Balsam, Arthur
Bardon, Mrs.
Barisič, Susan Hayes
Barrett, Stephen
Barzun, Mariana Lowell
Bateman, John
Bauman, C.
Baxter, Martha
de Beaucaron, Regnault
Becker, William
Behrend, Louise
Behrens, Hillary
Bein, Allen
Bein, Joseph
Bein, Robert
Belcher, Harold
Belmont, Peter
Belmont, Sibyl Totah
Bellows, Jerry
Benditt, Eleanor
Bendokas, Thirzah
Bennett, Bonnie
Bennett, David
Benoliel, Peter
Benton, Kate
Bera, Theodore
Berenblum, Doris
Berenson, Sharon
Berezi, Joseph

Berger, Father
Berger, Lucille
Bergfeld, Kricki
Bergonzi, Dante
Bestor, Dorothea
Beveridge, Lowell
Beveridge, Peter
Bevin, Elizabeth, P.
Binger, B.
Bishop, Mr.
Bizet, Miss
Blackman, Martha
Blankstein, Mary Freeman
de Blasius, Giovannina
de Blasius, Virginia
Blatt, Philip
Bleeker, Mrs. Paul
Bloch, Alexander
Bloch, Mr. & Mrs.
Bloch, Emil
Bloch, Eva
Bloch, Henry
Bloch, Hubert
Bloland, Susan Erikson
Bloomfield, Frances Aub
Boasson, Dorian
Boasson, Martha
Bodo, Andre
Boldini, Edmond
Bolles, Robert
Bond, Marie
Booth, Miss
Borges, Robert
Borneman, Alma
Botelho, Mr.
Bowen, Catherine Drinker
Boyer, Mr.

Boyet, H.
Brackman, Julia
Bram, Marjorie
Brandis, Matthias
Brant, Henry
Brasé, Nancy
Brecker, John
Breed, Elizabeth
Breger, Leo
Brehm, Alvin
Brenner, Joel
Bressler, Charles
Bretz, H.M.
Bridges, Ruth
Brill, David
Britt, C.
Britton, H.
Brockway, Katharine
Broekhuysen, William
Brogan, M.
Bromberg, Mr.
Bromberg, Pat
Brooks, Bobby
Brown, B.
Brown, Katherine
Brown, M.
Brummer, Mr.
de Bruyn, Gracia
Bry, Edwin
Bry, Mrs. Edwin
Buck, Carol
Bueding, Ernest
Buhler, Kurt
Buitikan, Mr. & Mrs.
Bulba, Susan
Bulla, Max
Bunting, Christopher
Burbano, Dr. Gabriel
Burbano, Mrs. Gabriel
Burnham, James
Burnham, John
Burnham, Toby
Burnham, William
Butler, Norman (Carver)
Buxtorf, Brigitte
Byrne, Patricia

Cable, Yvonne
Calvert, Celia
Campbell, Lady
Cantor, Jean
Calmeyer, Virginia
Carabella, Mr.
Carter, Helen
Cartwright, Margit
Cartwright, P.
Cartwright, Richard
Casanova, Miss
Castleman, Heidi
Cates, David
Cazeaux, Isabelle
Chalcroft, Mr. S.H.
Chancellor, Betty
Chancellor, Paul
Chapman, E.
Chapman, Harmon
Chase, Mrs. Stuart
Chassell, A.
Chatov, R.
Chelimsky, Samuel
Cherry, Jesse
Childs, Jack
Christ, Felix
Christy, Margaret
Christy, Mrs.
Chung, Myung Hee
Citrob, Dr.
Clark, Margaret
Clarke, Frieda
Clarke, Hans
Clarke, Rebecca
Clemons, Claire
Cochran, Mrs.
Cocilla, Barbara
Coffin, Ruth
Cogan, J.
Coggin, James
Coggleshall, Madge
Cohen, Laurence
Cohen, Sol
Cohn, Dr. Hans
Cohn, Waldo
Colburn, Lois
Coleman, Robert

Coletta, Harold
Colin, Mr. R.
Combs, Beatrice Mathews
Commanday, David
Conover,
   Mr. & Mrs. Herbert
Contos, Catherine
Converse, Connie
Cook, Ian
Cook, Nancy
Coolidge, John
Coolidge, Sprague
Coomara, Rohini
Coplin, Naomi
Corigliano, John
Costa, Mr.
Cotton, William
Covolo, G.
Coxe, Nigel
Coy, Dorothy
Coy, Virginia
Cramer, Hugh
Crena de Iongh,
   Polly Herter Norton
Crossley, Lou
Crouse, Mr.
Cunningham, Nicholas
Cunningham, Ruth
Currier, Mr.
Curwen, Ruth Miller
Curtis, Mr. R.

D'Archambeau, Pierre
Davis, Mrs.
Davison, Henry
Deering, Henri
De Gray, Julian
De Gray, Margaret
Delacorte, Margarita
Delmolino, Mrs.
De Miranda, Mr.
Denesuk, Mr.
Deri, Susan
De Ronde, Marion
Deschere, John
De Spur, Mr.
Dethier, Christine

183

Dethier, Edouard
Deveau, Betty
Di Bonventuro
Dietrich, Mr.
Di Marco, Miss
Dober, Lee Lyman
Dodge, Anne
Dodge, d'Etta
Dodge, Polly
Dodge, Sally
Dolan, Mrs.
Donahue, Miss
Donner, Madge
Dougal, Julie
Down, Betty Barbour
Driggs, Carol
Driggs, Louise
Driggs, Marshall
Dritell, Anna
Ducloux, Walter
Dunham, Charlotte
Dunham, James
Dupony, Jean
Durand, Auguste
Durand, Robert
Durieux, William

Earnshaw, K.
East, Peter
Edelberg, Alicia
Edwards, Marjorie
Ehrlich, Jesse
Eichwald, Dr.
Eisenstein, Anne
Eksergian
Elder, Mr.
Eldot, Charlotte
Elias, Anthony
Ellis, Mildred
Emerson,
   Ann McCollester
Emerson, Jeanette
Engeler, Eugène
Engelhard, George
Engler, Alan
Ensign, Judith
Erickson, Vivi

Erle, Broadus
Eseman, Mr.
Eshelman, Mr.
Evans, Margie Cree
Evans, Mrs. Jacob
Extermann, A.
Extermann, Philip
Extermann,
   Mr. & Mrs. Richard

Fagin, Gary
Fain, Miss
Fairchild, Mary
Farbman, Aaron
Feher, George
Feingold, Mr.
Feldman, Robert
Ferrante, Joan
Ferree, Russell
Finckel, George
Fine, Mr. & Mrs. Burton
Fink, Louis
Finkelstein, N.
Fippen, Cheryl
Fischer, Mrs.
Fishbein, Robert
Fishman, Alan
Flanders, Kathy
Flanders, Peter
Flanders, Tamzen
Fleisig, Calman
Fletcher, Katy
Forbes, Charles
Ford, Clinton
Ford, Mrs. J.H.
Forte, Miss
Fotino, Serban
Foy, Katharine
Frager, Malcolm
Francis, Marcia
Frank, Paul
Freeman, Florence
Freeman, Henry
Freeman, Robert
Freeman, Ruth
Friedland, Gladys
Frisch, Albert

Froelich, Ralph
Fromageot, Mr. & Mrs.
Frost, Mr.
Fry, Louise
Fryer, Judith
Fryxell, M.
Fryxell, Robert
Fuchs, Mr. C.
Fuchs, H.
Fund, Mr.
Fyffe, Mr.

Gabbe, Harald
Gallet, Anne
Gardner, Lois
Gardner, Lucille
Garniez, Nancy
Garrison, Sarah Crocker
Garth, Helen
Gasparian, Mr.
Gauger, Ted
Gehr, Ronnie
Gelley, Alex
Gershman, Paul
Gerstenberger,
   Martha Field
Gex, Beth
Gibbs, Edward
Gibian, Richard
Gibson, Mr.
Glazer, David
Goberman, Jean
Goberman, John
Goldberg, Maud
Goldman, Roberta
Goldmark, Peter
Goldschmidt, Otto
Goldstein, David
Gollancz, Livia
Golton, Estelle
Gomez, Miss H.
Goodkind, Herbert
Goodkind, John
Gordon, Cora
Gorrill, Sterling
Gorsira, Eric
Gorsira, Louise

Gottlieb, Sidney
Gould, Eleanor
Granitsas, Mrs.
Grau, Alfred
Greber, C.
Grebler, Leo
Gregor, Mr. & Mrs.
Green, Mr.
Greenberg, Nina
Greenebaum, Linda
Greenebaum, Michael
Greenfield, Mr. & Mrs. E.W.
Grier, Miss A.
Griggs, Louise McGregor
Groetzer, David
Grokoest, Albert
Grosgurin, Daniel
Grueninger, Walter
Gummer, Phyllis
Guthrie, Martha
Gutmacher, Eileen
Gutmacher, John
Guy, Mr.

Hadley, Emily
Hagenah, Elizabeth
Hagler, Mildred
Halik, Carolyn
Hall, William
Halpert, Edward
Handel, Mr. & Mrs.
Hansen, Einar
Harding, Catherine
Harding, Mason
Harding, Steven
Harding, Thomas
Hartman, Milton
Hartshorne, Mimi
de Harven, Dr.
Harzanyi, Mr.
Haskins, Margaret
Hathaway, Ron
Hayden, Mary
Hayden, William
Hayes, A.M.
Hayes, Samuel
Hegyi, Mr. & Mrs. Julius

Heidelberger, Charlotte
Heidelberger, Michael
Heinen, Barbara
Heller, Walter
Helsen, Dr.
Helsen, Ravenna
Hendrickson, Frances
Henkin, Saul
Henry, Harold
Hertig, Renée
Hilkert, Robert
Hill, John
Hilligos, Mr.
Hills, Mrs.
Hirsch, Helen
Hoff, Mrs.
Hoffman, Irwin
Hofmeester, Jeanette
Hokanson, L.
Hollander, Max
Holmes, Malcolm
Hood, Miss
Hoover, Edgar
Horan, Damaris Smith
Hornbostle, Anna
Horne, Grant
Horowitz, Dorothy
Hough, Nancy
Howorth, Denise
Humphrey, George
Hunkins,
  Mr. & Mrs. Sterling
Huntington, Francis
Hurwitz, David
Hurwitz, Isaac
Hurwitz, Jane
Hurwitz, Ruth
Hussid, Mrs.
Hutchins, Carleen
Hyde, Fred
Hyman, Robert
Ides,
  Mr. & Mrs. Pimenedes
Irmiger, Anne Marie

Jacobi, Irene
Jacobs, Bertram

Jacobs, Veronica
Jacobs, Zalik
Jacobson, Glenn
Jaffee, Martha
James, Henry
James, Peggy Spencer
James, Rosemary
Jamison, Robert
Johnson, A.R.
Johnson, Ogden
Jones, Sue Coolidge
Jorquera, Carlos
Joseph, Harry
Just, Mrs.
Jütte,
  Mr. & Mrs. Gerhard

Kahn, Gordon
Kalick, Dr.
Kalish, Gilbert
Kalish, Robert
Kalmar, George
Karrick, Elizabeth
Kartman, Myron
Katz, Miss
Katzen, Bernard
Kautzman,
  Mr. & Mrs. Daniel
Keats, Sheila
Keen, Ben
Keilmann, Mrs.
Keitel, Hans
Keller, Mr.
Kellert, Marjorie
Kemper, Ruth
Kendall, Mrs. S.
Kennedy, Marjorie
Kennedy, Mrs. R.
Kent, Dorothy
Kent, Mrs.
Kenton, Egon
Kernochan, John
Kieransky, Elizabeth
Kimball, Maulsby
Kindler, R.
Kingman, Lucius
Kingman, Russell

Klein, Eric
Klemperer, Carol
Klemperer, Mr.
Klensch, Prof. & Mrs.
Kloos, Dr.
Knafo, Ellen
Kneisel, Frank
Knight, Margaret
Knight, Mr. E.
Knopf, Alfred
Kobrak, Gerhard
Koenigsberger,
  Alice Kortschak
Koerber, Mr.
Koller, Mr.
Kornbliet, Irving
Korst, Mrs.
Kotlarsky, Serge
Kougell, Maurice
Kraft, Mr.
Krejci, Jan
Kroll, William
Krosnick, Dr.
Krosnick, Joel
Kroyt, Claire
Kuerti, Anton
Kunhardt, Keith
Kuskin, Larry

Lachenbruch, Morton
Lambert, George
Lander, Rose
La Porte, Mary Jones
Larssen, Mr. H.
Lash, Mr. & Mrs. Irving
Lasker, H.
Lauterberg, Anne Marie
Lawner, Alice
Lawton, Dr.
Lawton, Jane
Leavitt, Hart
Lee, Isidore
Lee, Jeong
Leedy, Mr. & Mrs. Dino
Legge, Mary Gray
Lehmann, Eleanor S.
Lehmann, Pedro A.

Lehner, Andreas
Lehner, Eugene
Lehrer, Eleanor Benditt
Lemay, Paul
Levine, Julius
Levinson, Mr.
Levite, Myron
Levy, Barbara
Levy, Hyman
Levy, Jack
Leyburn, J.
Liebling, Walter
Lifschey, Samuel
Limberg, Eugenie
Linder, Felix
Linglebach, Barbara
Lipcon, Dora
Lipkin, Arthur Bennett
Lipsky, Mrs. Alexander
Little, Dorothy Fay
Little, Dwight
Littlehales, Lillian
Llewellyn, Ernest
Lloyd, Mr.
Lloyd, Robert
Lloyd, Susan McIntosh
Lobb, Nancy
Lockhart, Lee
Loeb, Elizabeth
Loeb, Ellen
Loeb, John
Loewendahl, Ben
Loewendahl,
  Daphne Spottiswoode
Loewendahl, David
Loewy,
  Mr. & Mrs. Richard
Loft, Jacob
Lomolino, Francis
Longo, Janice
Loukin, Lucile
Lowell, Elizabeth
Luce, Ingrid
Lynn, Eric
Lyon, Mr.
Lyon, Will
Lyons, Lisa Sandow

Lywen, Werner

Ma, Yeou Cheng
Maas, Robert
MacDonald, Helen
MacDonald,
  Kay Johnson
MacDonald, S.
Macomber
Madden, Betty
Maguire, Robert
Mailman, Alma
Makman, Maynard
Makman, M.H.
Makman, Richard
Malkevitch, Nina
Mamelock, Alfred
Mankewitz, Eugenia
Marantz, Fred
Marcus, Alfred
Marcus, Peter
Margolius, Mary
Marston, Liane
Martin, Jean
Martin, Judith
Martin, Susan
Martori, Frank
Marx, Madelena
Mason, Mrs.
Mather, Caroline
Mayer, Ellen
Mayer, Steven
McAdams, Martha
McAvoy, Clifford
McCann, Christine
McCann, Ruth
McClellan, James
McCollester, Dorna
McCollester, Parker
McDowell, Jack
McDowell, Ruth
McGhee, Hildegund
McGhee, Steve
McGill, Dr.
McGregor, David
McGregor, Ruth Hill
McIntosh, Beth

McIntosh, Carey
McIntosh, Craig
McIntosh, James
McIntosh, Kenneth
McIntosh, Margaret
McIntosh, Mimi
McIntosh, Nadia
McIntosh, Richard
McIntosh, Rob
McIntosh, Rustin
McKinley, Ethel
McLinden, Ladd
McNichols, Mrs.
Mengers, Mr.
Mention, M.
Merriam, Mrs.
Merrick, Miss
Merrill, Winifred
Meyer, Harry
Meyer, Henry
Middlemiss, Jean
Milch, Dr.
Milford, K.
Miller, Robert
Mills, Catherine
Mills, Margaret
Miner, G.
Minty, Dorothy
Mishakoff, Ann
Mitchell, Jean
Modern, Geraldo
Moerschel, Joel
Moerschel, Rita
Mohr, Jenny
Mok, Robert
Monosoff, Sonya
Montgomery, John
Moore, E.
Moraga, Mario
Morgan, Carlyle
Morgan, Helen
Morgenstern, Elvira
Morgenstern, Marvin
Morrison, Ralph
Moss, Gail
Moss, Paul
Munang, Alice

Myer, Dr. H.
Myers, Gordon
Myrvaagnes, Eric
Myrvaagnes,
    Naomi Suconick

Nastasi, Roy
Neidich, Charles
Neidich, Irving
Neill, A.
Neizert, George
Neubauer, Ernst
Newbury, Miss
Newman, Brian
Newman, Cela
Newman, Ruby
Newmark, Jonathan
Newton, Abby
Newton, Nan
Nicholson, Graham
Nolte, Virginia
Norfleet, Katharine
North, Gladys
Norton, Sonya Spencer
Nott,
    Mr. & Mrs. Malcolm
Nussbaum, Isadore

Ocko, Bernard
O'Neal, Mr. S.
Oppenheimer, Mr.
Ortenzi, Teresina
Osius, Richard
O'Steen, Alton
Ostroff, Esther
Ouvry, Mr.

Pabst, S.
Paddock, Marjorie
Palmer,
    Francesca Gilder
Pancaldo, Ariana
Pancaldo, Dina
Pancaldo, Mia
Pancaldo, Susan
Pappenheimer,
    Dr. & Mrs. A.M., Sr.

Pappenheimer,
    Alwin M., Jr.
Pappenheimer, Hylie
Pappenheimer, John
Pappenheimer, Sally
Paret, Helen
Paret, Henry
Parker, Lucy
Payne, Aileen Webster
Payne, Elizabeth
Payne, Roger
Pearce, Suzanne Schell
Pearson, Florence
Pearson, Robert
Penney, Barbara
Pernel, Orrea
Peterkin, John
Peterson, V.
Philibosian, Aida
Pickering, Norman
Pierce, Mr.
Pierce, Nancy
Pietropoulo, Mrs.
Pimenedes, Mrs.
Pitman, Cecilia
Piston, Mr.
Pitney, Robert
Pivar, Stuart
Plascek, Adolf
Pledge, Gene
Polk, Dorothy
Pollak, Mr.
Pollakis, Chris
Ponsi, Miss M.
Porter, Ingrid
Posner, Erica
Posner, Larry
Posner, Rose
Posnett, Mrs.
Post, Mrs. O.G.
Potter, H.
Potter, Ruth
Powell, Homer
Powell, Mr. W.
Prager, B.
Pruyn, Laura Louise
Pugh, Nansi

Purcell, Grace Ann
Purvin, Herbert
Purvin, Jonathan
Purvin, Louise
Pushman, Armand
Putman, Raymond

Rabin, Ed
Radić, Stjepan
Rahm, Barbara
Rahn, Mr. H.
Raimondi, Matthew
Raisbeck, Gordon
Ravetti, Odette
Rayment, Mrs.
Recket, Natalie
Rector, Margaret
Redfield, S.
Reicher, Thomas
Reichler, Vera
Reid, Betsy Aub
Relkin, Nathan
Remze, Paul
Rex, Barbara
Rex, Theodore
Rhein, William
Ricco, Fritz
Ricci, George
RICE, HELEN
Rice, Edwin T.
Richards, Connie
Richardson, Margie
Richmond, Gordon
Richter,
  Mr. & Mrs. Alexander
Ring, Alden
Ripley, Virginia
Ripple, Louise Herron
Ristorcelli,
  Dorothy Averill
Robbins, Norman
Robeson, Mr.
Robins, Pat
Robinson, Bernard
Robison, M.
Robitaille, Mr.
Roedenberg, Andriés

Rogers, Mr. J.M.
Rogers, Patsy
Rood, Louise
Rose, Hannah
Rose, Kip
Rosen, Elmer
Rosen, Mr. & Mrs.
Rosenfeld, Elizabeth
Rosenfeld, Jay
Rosenfeld, Peter
Rosenfeld, Stephen
Rosenwald,
  Mrs. William
Ross, Charles
Rossmassler, Elfreda
Rossoff, Mr.
Rothen, Alexandre
Rothen, Genevieve
Roubound, Miss
Roudebush, Francis
Rowe, Judith
Rozek, R.
Rubenstein, Ann Little
Rubenstein, Bernard
Rubenstein, Harry
Rubin, Alida
Rubin, David
Rudiakov, Michael
Rudo, Mr.
Rudoff, Patricia Leland
Rushton,
  Dr. & Mrs. William
Russell, Alfred
Russell, John

Sachs, I.
Sackson, David
Sahli, Anne-Tillie
Sahli, Isabelle
Saltonstall,
  Cecilia Drinker
Samaroff, Toscha
Sampson, George
Samson, Ilan
Sandberg, Melba
Sandler, Emily
Sanford, Mr. C.

Saperstein, Bernice
Sass, M.
Saunders, Frederick
Schaaf, Joseph
Schaefer, Lois
Schaller, William
Schector, Sam
Schector, David
Schauffler,
  Robert Haven
Schell,
  Betsy Frederick
Schelling, Mr.
Schenkman, Edgar
Schenkman,
  Marguerite
Scherer, Alex
Scherer, Zena
Schickele, David
Schier, Miss
Schimel, Albert
Schleicher, Verena
Schlesinger, Miss
Schlesinger, Walter
Schmid, A.
Schmitt, Dr.
Schnitzler, Mrs.
Schrade, Robelyn
Schrade, Robert
Schroeder, Gay
Schroeder, Svend
Scoville, Laura
Schuman, Henry
Schwab, Edith
Schwartzbart, Harry
Schwarz, Otto
Schwarz, Sanford
Sears, John
Secunda, Daniel
Seigel,
  Jayn Rosenfeld
Seigel, Jerrold
Seitz, Ted
Seward, Mr.
Sharp, Miss A.M.
Shaw, Leora
Shaw, Morris

Shaw, Thomas Mott
Sheff, Henrietta
Sheffer, Jonathan
Shelton, Lucy
Shelton, Nancy
Sherrard, Edward
Shotler, Mr.
Shure, Mr.
Silver, Herman
Simenauer, Lothar
Simenauer, Peter
Simmel, Arnold
Simmons, Mrs.
Simon, Henry
Singer, Gregory
Singer, Jack
Singer, Laurie
Singer, Max
Skeist, Irving
Skemer, Peggy Stein
Sly, Allan
Sly, Betty
Sly, Caroline
Small, Charles
Smiley, Alice
Smith, Carlton Sprague
Smith, Doris Doehler
Smith, Ellen
Smith, Ethel
Smith, Florence Duvall
Smith, Hannah Coffin
Smith, Julia
Smith, M.T.
Snow, Emma
Snow, Richard
Snyder, Lee
Snyder, Sandra
Sokoloff, William
Solmssen, Mimi
Sorkin, Herbert
Spencer, D.
Spencer, Mrs.
Spencer, Sandy
Spohr, Mr.
Spring, Mr.
Spring, Mrs. G.
Spuehler, Donald

Spuehler, Jane
Stapelfeldt, Karsten
Stark, M.
Stein, Andy
Stein, Carol
Stein, Elzy
Stein, Ernest
Stein, Fred
Stein, Joseph
Stein, Josie
Stein, Lise
Stein, Ludwig
Steinberg, J.
Steinberg, Mr.
Stern, Carl
Stern, J.
Stern, Mr. & Mrs. J.
Stevens, George
Sticherling, Angelica
Stocker, Markus
Stocklinski, Jan
Stocklinski, Marjorie
Stoffel, Ronald
Stojowski, Mrs.
Stott, Gordon
Straight, Mr.
Strauss, Gerald
Strauss, Gideon
Strauss, Leonard
Stuckens, Leo
Strong, Peter
Sturges, Pemberton
Stwertka, Mr.
Sullivan, Walter
Sumner, Sarah
Swan, Verne
Swann, Mabel
Swatsler, Lucinda Breed
Swett, Sally
Swing, Peter
Swing, Timothy
Szlachta, Wieslaw
Szigeti, Joseph

Taber, Helen
Tangeman, Clementine
Tarak, Arturo

Tarlow, Mark
Tartakoff, Alan
Tartakoff, David
Tatar, Clara
Taussig, Chris
Taylor, Lawrence
Teegen, Otto
Temmer, Mrs.
Tempia, Alain
Tennen, Denise
Tennen, Hannah
Tennen, Robert
Thomas, Carol Bedell
Thomas, Mr. R.
Thomas, William
Torchun, Mr.
Totenburg, Roman
Toulmin, Libby
Toumanoff, Prince
Trampler, Walter
Treat, Asher
Tregel-Reznicek, Miss
Treml, Josephine
Truedson, Mr.
Tuma, Liz
Tuttle, Karen

Ulanowsky, Paul
Underwood, Margaret
Urban, Eva
Usher, Sara

Vagenheim, Mrs.
Van Doren, Mrs.
Vashaw, Cecile
Vaska, Bedrich
Vielehr, Mrs.
Vinograde, Jan
Viret, M.
Vogel, Barbara Baird
Vogel, Manfred
Vollenweider, Carlos
Vollm, Klaus

Wade, Morris
Wade, Mrs.
Wahl, Annie

Walcott, Martha
Wallis, Joan
Wanamaker, Margaret
Wang, Alfredo
Ward, Ann Richards
Ward, John
Ward, Robert
Ward, Susan Ripley
Warfield, Marguerite
Warren, Winifred Merrill
Watson, Sarah Ruth
Webster, Michael
Weinberg, Mr. N.
Weinstock, Rachmael
Weiser, Max
Weiss, Bert
Weisberg, Arthur
Weitzmann, Lee
Welch, Carol
Werchman, Ruth
Westling, H.
Westphal, Barbara

Wheeler, Eunice
White, J.
Whitman, Marianne
Whitney, Mr. H.
Wilde, Jean
Will, Christopher
Willeke, Sally
Williams, Betty
Williams, Carl
Williams, Miss
Williams, Mr. T.
Williams, Thomas
Wilson, Charles
Wilson, Jane Stein
Wilson, Mary
Wingreen, Harriet
Winternitz, William
Wire, Dorothy
Wittenburg, Dr.
Wohl, Alice Sedgwick
Wohl, Hellmut

Wolf, Paul
Wolfsohn, Mr. N.
Wollman, Mr.
Wood, Trudy
Woodruff,
   Lucia Norton
Woolworth, Mildred
Wright, Ashley
Wright, Catherine

Yannatos, James
Yellin, Florence
Yeomans, Edward
Young, Mr.

Zentall, Kate
Zentrick, Mr.
Zeritzky, Samuel
Zighera, Alfred
Zirner, Ludwig
Zuch, Sue
Zulack, Mary Marsh

PICTURE CREDITS (where known)

Almost all of the pictures used throughout the text of the biography and the letter section were found in Helen's Stockbridge house. In many cases it was impossible to know who had taken them. We regret not being able to credit these various photographers. If you will identify yourselves to our ACMP Editor*, giving description and page number, we will gladly publish in our next ACMP Newsletter the names of these people to whom we are indebted.

> * ACMP, Inc.
> 633 E Street NW
> Washington, DC 20004

191